HURRICANES
VERSUS
ZEROS

Air Battles over
Java, Sumatra and Singapore

HURRICANES
VERSUS
ZEROS

Air Battles over
Java, Sumatra and Singapore

by
Terence Kelly

Pen & Sword
AVIATION

To our great grand-daughter
Nia
With all our love
Ann and Terence

First published in Great Britain in 1985 by Robert Hale Ltd,
under the title *Battle For Palembang*

Published in 2007 in this format by
PEN & SWORD AVIATION
an imprint of
Pen & Sword Books Ltd
47 Church Street
Barnsley
South Yorkshire
S70 2AS

Copyright © Terence Kelly, 1985, 2007

ISBN 978-1-84415-622-1

The right of Terence Kelly to be identified as Author
of this work has been asserted by him in accordance
with the Copyright, Designs and Patents Act 1988.

Printed and bound in Great Britain by
CPI UK

Pen & Sword Books Ltd incorporates the Imprints of
Pen & Sword Aviation, Pen & Sword Maritime, Pen & Sword Military,
Wharncliffe Local History, Pen & Sword Select,
Pen & Sword Military Classics and Leo Cooper.

For a complete list of Pen & Sword titles please contact:
PEN & SWORD BOOKS LIMITED
47 Church Street, Barnsley, South Yorkshire, S70 2AS, England
E-mail: enquiries@pen-and-sword.co.uk
Website: www.pen-and-sword.co.uk

Contents

List of Illustrations

viii

List of Maps

Dedication
and
Acknowledgements

This book is dedicated to all those men and women who, more than forty years ago, were caught up in the brief Sumatran Campaign but especially to pilots and ground crews of the RAF and RAAF fighter and bomber squadrons who offered the major resistance to the Japanese, to the men of the Dutch Bofors Battery and the 12th Battery 6th Regiment Heavy Anti-Aircraft based at P.1 airfield and Pladjoe oil refinery who fought bravely, to the Maréchausée who were local native troops *par excellence*, to the captains and crews of the small ships who evacuated large numbers of men, women and children from stricken Singapore and to those who so successfully organized the escape of such of the latter as managed to evade the attacks of the aircraft and ships of the huge Japanese fleet which lay athwart their path.

It is from amongst these that most acknowledgements are due. Firstly there are the pilots, ground defence and ground staff who took part in the various actions related and who, like others who follow, were kind enough to supply me from all over the world with tapes, letters, notes and photographs. The list is long: Air Marshal Sir Harold Maguire, John A. ('Red') Campbell, 'Bertie' Lambert, 'Doug' Nichols, Campbell White, 'Herb' Plenty, Martin Ofield, Hedley Bonnes, Tom Jackson, Ambrose Milnes, 'Denny' Sharp, 'Bill' Taute, 'Ted' Ravenscroft, 'Ted' Smith, 'Des' Timmins, 'Soapy' Hudson, 'Bob' Chapman, John Vibert, Martyn Lovejoy and Arthur Sheerin. Army personnel who were involved in fighting the Japanese to whom I should also like to send my thanks are Bombardier F. East, Mr A.H.C.Roberts, Eric Rice, Mr A.N.Simpson and Mr G.W.Jones whilst amongst those who were at sea are Commander Len Cooper, Lieutenant Smythe and the Revd Eric Sinclair. I am grateful to many others who have helped me including 'Bill' Belford, 'Syd' Lewis, Andrew Mills, Mr M. Cullerton, Eric Horton, Norman Chick, 'Perce' Wellington, 'Jim' Home, Harold Pearce, and 'Pete' Robins. My very special thanks go to Donald Wright for the marvellous story of his escape and to Philip de Leon who has been to enormous trouble on my behalf and Mr J.J.Jiskoot to whom he introduced me, nor would the list be complete without mentioning Denis Russell-Roberts whose splendid book *Spotlight on Singapore* is a *must* for anyone interested in this area. Other writers whose work has been most helpful include Lionel Wigmore (*The Japanese Thrust*), Yasuo Izawa (*Combat Diary of the 64th Sentai*) and David Thomas (*The Battle of the Java Sea*). Nor would it do to neglect to thank the Imperial War Museum who go to so much trouble trying to dredge up photographs of a campaign where few had cameras (and those who did lost practically everything to the Japanese) and the many Far East Prisoner of War Associations who have been so helpful in my search for information. Finally, may I apologize to any I have missed who should have been listed and assure them that all information received, however slight its content, has been taken into account and has helped to fashion this book. Thank you.

Foreword by
Air Marshal Sir Harold Maguire
KCB, DSO, OBE

As well as the accounts from Allied military historians, who in general have tended to skim over the Sumatran Campaign, there have been books and articles in plenty about individual or group experiences in the post-Singapore débâcle, many centring on escapes from Sumatra. But this is a story of a different kind. Terence Kelly has endeavoured to chronicle the events which took place in February 1942, in the vital area around Palembang from many points of view. He includes those of the Dutch, the Japanese, and in more detail, the British forces which were engaged. He also covers the wider issue of the military and economic importance of the whole island to both sides. He speculates on the possible outcome of a more successfully protracted defence against what is now seen to be an inconsiderable attacking force.

Apart from his ability as a writer, Terence Kelly is well qualified to do this task. His research has been meticulous, his interest unflagging, after all he was there, and he has shown commendable zeal in his efforts to track down and interview survivors. He has produced a narrative which is in my view unique. The end result has been to stimulate and record the memories of many events which occurred forty-two years ago and to provide a document which should serve as a mine of information for future historians.

Preface

Important military events can be so overshadowed by others of greater moment and notoriety that they scarcely find their way into the history books – and so it was with the battle for Palembang.

Palembang lies approximately one sixth of the way up Sumatra, the fifth largest island in the world which straddles the Equator, dwarfs its eastern neighbour, Malaya, and stretches for twelve hundred miles from the Nicobar Islands in the Bay of Bengal in the north, to Krakatoa and the westerly tip of Java in the south. This remarkable country is one of great contrasts, at once beautiful beyond belief and evil beyond words. To the west rises a tremendous mountain range twelve thousand feet in height and over this huge collecting area pour daily tropical downpours of phenomenal intensity forming great rivers which sweep down to the wide eastern plain which terminates in swamps almost unbroken for a thousand miles in length and in some parts more than a hundred miles in depth. Between mountain ridges and swamps the land is largely covered with jungle of such impenetrability that from the air nothing breaks its endless, unvarying green but the brown swathes of the mighty rivers which finally end in baffling deltas where they pour into the Malacca Straits and the South China and Java Seas. It is a country of few roads and railways, sparsely populated, containing huge areas even to this day virtually unexplored, inhabited by wild animals and untamed tribes. It is a country plagued by disease: dysentery, cholera, typhoid, malaria, blackwater fever, dengue. From the gigantic mangrove and other swamps and in the dense, trackless jungles swarm mosquitoes, snakes and leeches in unconscionable numbers. The rivers, fast-flowing, chocolate-coloured from the teeming rain, abound with crocodiles, the sea with sharks; panthers and tigers roam the forests undisturbed.

In a word Sumatra is precisely that kind of country which presents the maximum problems to an invading force. Yet this huge country, strategically vital to the Japanese, rich in oil, coal, tin, bauxite, gold and silver, rubber, coffee, copra, tobacco, rice, was effectively taken by a relatively tiny force of Japanese in a matter of twenty-four hours without even token resistance from its masters, the Dutch. Palembang, straddling the mighty Moesi River, navigable to large craft for the seventy miles up to the town, was the key to Sumatra; and P.1, the airfield on which a squadron or so of Hurricanes was based, was the key to Palembang. The invasion was planned by the Japanese with scrupulous care. Approaching twenty thousand soldiers transported in a convoy of about thirty transports with supporting naval ships was to occupy Palembang and fan out north and south – but only after two initial objectives had been achieved: the first, the seizure of P.1 airfield and the Pladjoe oil refinery; the second the link-up with the paratroops by an advance force of about one thousand infantry travelling up three rivers. In the entire, carefully plotted plan, were contained no instructions as to what should happen if the paratroops were to fail in their initial objective.

And they very nearly failed. They were opposed not by regular infantry units but by a handful of Allied pilots – mainly American, Australian, British and New Zealanders – a small force of RAF groundstaff and defence men, a couple of anti-aircraft batteries and a few, quite magnificent, native troops. On the airfield the paratroops were held and bloody casualties were inflicted on the companies advancing up the rivers. It was only on instructions which, in turn, were based on muddle, confusion, incompetence and misinformation, that the men on the ground withdrew from an airfield yet to be taken from them and the pilots suspended the awful carnage they were wreaking on the rivers. They did as they were ordered and on 15 February, 1942, Palembang fell – as did Singapore.

The battle for Palembang was in the context of a major war, a tiny skirmish – but every man who was there that day can tell astonishing tales – tales which for courage, endurance, imagination and even humour match any other.

Battle for Palembang is more than an account of an incredible twenty-four hours for it covers all aspects of the Sumatran campaign: the Japanese planning, the massacre of the tiny ships from Singapore, the meticulously planned escape route through Sumatra for those considered too valuable to be taken prisoner, the brave efforts of a tiny air force hopelessly outnumbered, of ships hopelessly outgunned, the courage of ordinary men and women, the cowardice and confusion amongst some of their so-called leaders, the final headlong rout.

But central to this are just two days: 14 February and 15 February, 1942, which may justifiably lay claim to be as remarkable as any in the war.

Terence Kelly. Frieth 1985

Note: The spelling of place names creates some difficulty for not only were there alternatives at the time when the action of this book is set but, following independence from the Dutch, the Indonesian Government made further important changes as, for example, substituting *u* for *oe*. On the whole I have adopted the spelling which I believe was used at the time these events occurred; this spelling will not correspond exactly with that found, for example, on current maps.

1
The Japanese Story

Whereas most countries, even the defeated ones, retained accurate records of their wartime campaigns this does not apply in the case of Japan because the devastating bombing and the consequent fires which swept through Tokyo in the last few months of the Far East War destroyed most official Japanese records. Having discovered this to be the case, the Americans instructed their defeated foe to prepare what were to be known as 'historical monographs' covering the various fields of operations and it is from these that much of the material which reflects the Japanese view of the Sumatran Campaign has been drawn. While it is generally believed that the substance of these monographs represents the most accurate and reliable information available, it has to be borne in mind that much contained in them has been reconstructed from the memory of former officers in command or in staff units during the period of operations. It should also be remembered that these officers often had to rely upon the reports they received from the field as to how the campaigns were proceeding and particularly for the details of enemy losses.

Whilst I was a prisoner in Japan we were, for some of the time, supplied with copies of *The Nippon Times* which was a newspaper printed in English. The claims made of Allied ships sunk and aircraft destroyed were so exaggerated as, even to prisoners, to be patently absurd. To some degree no doubt these glaring exaggerations were intentionally printed for propaganda purposes, but it is also certain that the articles would have been influenced by highly coloured and over-optimistic reports from the battle fronts. Pilots, in particular, are prone to wishful thinking as has never been more clearly shown than by the comparison of claims made by Allied pilots in the Battle of Britain and official German results of losses incurred. An aircraft moves very swiftly and it is rare that a pilot can enjoy the luxury of circling the target area to cross-check his first impression of the effects of his bombing raid and when a fighter pilot believes he has achieved one combat victory his immediate concern is normally more for the possibility of another enemy's being on his tail than of watching his victim actually plunge into sea or jungle. It is clear from these monograms that the Japanese were equally as prone to wishful thinking as their Allied counterparts for, as will be seen, their claims for losses of aircraft in a single raid far exceeded the total number of machines actually on the airfield at any time (although, to be fair, one must add that to a degree they would have been deluded by wooden imitation aircraft strategically disposed), while, again, the Japanese accounts of the fighting exaggerate, to an almost ridiculous degree, the forces arraigned against them, create barracks which did not exist and refer to engagements which took place after all Allied troops had been evacuated.

Truth is elusive and the most diligent researcher can do no more than select out of the material available. In the pages which follow I will be quoting verbatim or drawing from applicable Japanese monographs even though these may in parts be *prima facie* exaggerated, self-contradictory or even absurd, because these are the best sources from which to promote the Japanese point of view. So far as the events were observed from an Allied standpoint, I shall be selecting, from a wealth of reports, material which seems to me not to be knowingly falsified and best accords with the facts I know to be correct from personal experience. Much will be conflicting but, unless I am prepared to set myself up as sole judge and arbiter, this is unavoidable. However, just as twenty criticisms of a play, however varied, give a far better idea of its quality and content than one however genuinely and carefully prepared, so, I am optimistic enough to believe, will the many contradictory views, opinions and experiences which follow give a better picture of the events of a few remarkable days which occurred more than forty years ago than could be obtained by ruthless

A portion of the Far East Asia War Theatre.

pruning of any contribution which was at all suspect.

The decision to attack Palembang was taken by the Japanese early in January 1942 with the 38th Division commanded by Tadayoshi Sano entrusted with the operation. The division left Hong Kong on 20 January advancing to Camranh Bay, in what was at the time French Indo-China, where it joined up with attached units under the protection of formidable naval resources.

The plan called for the 1st Parachute Brigade to seize P.1, as the airfield serving Palembang was known, and the nearby Pladjoe oil refinery, on a date yet to be decided (but referred to *pro tem* as 'X' Day minus one) and an Advance Force commanded by Colonel Tanaka, consisting of seven infantry companies with artillery, engineering and medical support, to precede the main body of the division. Two of these companies would attack Muntok on Banka (a large island lying to the east of Sumatra) at midnight of 'X' Day minus one, one company to seize and hold the nearby airfield while the other would advance and take Pangkalpinang some sixty or so miles away close to Banka's east coast. On 'X' Day the balance of the Advance Force, reinforced as soon as possible by such troops as were not engaged in taking Pangkalpinang or in securing Muntok, was to invade Sumatra with troops carried in self-propelled invasion barges travelling up the Moesi, Salang and Telang Rivers and join up with the airborne forces; the major effort was to be up the Moesi with three infantry companies and one mountain artillery company involved while one infantry company only would move up each of the other two.

Meanwhile the main body of the 38th Division, carried in twenty-eight transports, was to be heading for the mouth of the Moesi River which serves Palembang to reach there on 'X' Day Plus Two and move directly up the river at high tide to Palembang itself. After landing the division was to assist, if necessary, in the capture of Tandjoengkarang (otherwise known as Oosthaven), secure the oilfields near Palembang, occupy Bencoolen on the west coast and prepare for a drive on the oilfields at Djambi to the north. If these objectives were achieved, the Japanese would have secured the entire southern portion of Sumatra and its invaluable oilfields and could comfortably leave the larger balance of Sumatra cut off and ready to fall like a ripe plum once Singapore had been taken.

The first positive step in the invasion of Sumatra was a bombing raid on 23 January on the airfield at Palembang – P.1 – carried out from captured bases in North Malaya. The attack was made just after midday by twenty-seven bombers with fighter cover. According to the monogram the raid was intercepted by fifteen Allied fighters of which five were shot down and one burned on the ground whilst damage was caused to fourteen Japanese planes.

There followed over the next three weeks a series of bombing and strafing raids on P.1 in an attempt to destroy, or at least neutralize Allied air forces by 'X' Plus One Day – 11 February. However the original 'X' Day was delayed to the 15th at the request of the Navy and thus the paratroop drop planned for 9 February actually took place on the 14th.

General Imamura signs the surrender of the entire Japanese south-east Asia Army on board aircraft carrier HMS *Glory* off Rabaul on September 6th, 1945.

The operation (which bore the nomenclature 'L' Operation) was a combined Army and Navy affair with the Fleet under the command of Vice-Admiral Jizaburo Ozawa, the Army under Lt-Genl Hitoshi Imamura and the 3rd Air Group under Lt-Genl Michio Sugawara. The possibility of enforced delay through progress of the initial air operations, bad weather conditions or the discovery that the enemy strength might be other than supposed was taken into account and the Naval and Army Commanders were under instructions to agree, if necessary, a new 'X' Day by midday of 4 February. So far as the air operation was concerned Imamura was under instruction to consult with Sugawara.

The combined air forces to be employed and which were to operate from numerous captured airfields in Malaya and Borneo were strictly defined. Under naval command there would be approximately a hundred bombers, thirty fighters, six land-based reconnaissance planes and forty seaplanes; under army control there would be fifty bombers, seventy fighters and nine 'attack' planes – a total of three hundred and five aircraft whose losses could, no doubt, be made good if felt necessary. It is perhaps worth mentioning at this point that to the writer's certain knowledge the maximum number of fighters the Allies ever got into the air at any one time in Sumatra was fourteen – and those on the very morning the paratroops were dropped.

On two occasions 'X' Day was changed but 15 February having been finally decided upon, the raids to neutralize P.1 were put in hand. The Japanese versions of these various raids will be included later in their appropriate chronological locations.

The attack on Palembang was planned with great care and with complete confidence that the forces provided would be sufficient and success was assured. Although the paratroop drops (which were seen to be a vital ingredient) were to comprise a total of only four hundred and sixty men, no provision was made for reinforcing them. So far as calculations of the likely forces available to oppose them were concerned it would appear that the Japanese had been provided with information from collaborators but that this information was fairly sketchy. The total assessment given was: 'two to three infantry companies with four or five light tanks, machine guns and several infantry guns, several anti-aircraft guns and several planes'. The glaring mistake made by the Japanese which led them to underestimate the Allied air forces still remaining was their failure to discover a second airfield some forty miles to the south-west of Palembang which was known as P.2. It is clear there were firm suspicions that another airfield did exist but its probable location was badly misplaced for the documents state that it was 'said to be located between the north airfield (P.1) and Palembang'. This is, in fact, a curious suggestion, for had P.2 been so located, its circuit would, under the prevailing weather conditions, have been dangerously close to the circuit at P.1 and, anyway, it could hardly have been missed by a number of the many Japanese pilots who raided P.1.

At all events, miraculously, P.2 was not discovered and, as will be seen, was to prove a vital base from which the spirited resistance by the RAF and RAAF bomber and fighter squadrons against the overwhelming Japanese forces could be maintained at great cost to the enemy.

2
The RAF Moves In

On 29 January, 1942 thirteen Hurricanes of No 258 Squadron RAF took off from Kemajoran Airport in what was then Batavia, and is now Djkarta, to fly to Seletar Airfield, Singapore, making a refuelling stop *en route* at P.2. These thirteen aircraft were part of the first batch of sixteen out of a total of forty-eight Hurricanes which were to take off in three batches from HMS aircraft-carrier *Indomitable* from a position some three hundred miles south-west of Java. Through faulty

HMS *Indomitable* in the Indian Ocean.

brakes three of the first batch had overshot the Kemajoran runway and were badly damaged and at P.2 two more, landing across deep ruts left by Flying Fortresses taxiing on this rough and ready jungle airfield, came to grief.

After refuelling the remaining eleven flew up to Singapore but could not go into service until 31 January as on inspection it was discovered that their guns were caked in thick grease and (according to the armourers) had they been fired the wings would probably have been blown off. The first squadron scramble took place on the 31st when eight Hurricanes encountered enemy forces outnumbering them about ten to one, shot down a bomber and a fighter and lost two of their own shot down while three more were damaged. One of the squadron's New Zealand pilots, Bruce McAlister, was killed.

The eleven machines of 258 Squadron were not the first Hurricanes to arrive in Singapore for on 13 January twenty-four pilots made up of six each of the pilots of Nos 17, 135, 136 and 232 Squadrons had been diverted from a convoy containing the full complements of these four squadrons which were bound for the Middle East. The mixture was designated 232 Squadron and supplied with 51 Hurricane IIBs carried on another ship. Certain other pilots who were for one reason or another already in Singapore were also attached to the squadron and, meanwhile, the balance of the original 232 squadron (eighteen pilots) plus half a dozen others were on their way aboard *Indomitable*. On 29 January the latter, together with the remaining eight 258 squadron pilots took off *Indomitable* for Kemajoran Airport. Meanwhile HMS *Athene* transporting a further forty or fifty Hurricanes was steaming towards Java.

Thus it will be seen that by waiting until all aircraft were serviceable it would theoretically have been possible to put no less than ninety-six Hurricanes into the air at once with a back-up of perhaps fifty more machines. However this was not attempted. Pilots and machines were ordered up as and when available and, almost invariably meeting far larger formations whilst still, through inadequate warning of the enemy's approach, desperately climbing, were dribbled away in penny numbers. By the time the initial eleven Hurricanes of 258 Squadron arrived, out of the original twenty-four 232 Squadron

Hurricanes taxiing to stern of HMS *Indomitable*.

pilots nine had been killed and four so badly wounded as to have been shipped away, whilst in the process at least twenty-one Hurricanes had been lost and many more damaged to a smaller or a lesser degree.

It was fairly clear by now that Singapore would fall but the process of ferrying further pilots from 232 and 258 Squadrons up to Singapore using P.2 as a staging post continued and further losses both in action and through accident, and especially through accidents caused by P.2's soft terrain, occurred.

Following an unexplained muddle causing the abortion of an intended offensive raid on a up-country enemy-occupied airfield in Malaya on 3 February, all but four or five of 258's Hurricanes withdrew to the civilian airport at Palembang, known as P.1, while eleven of the newly arrived 232 Squadron pilots off *Indomitable* flew up to Singapore in Hurricanes and five more as passengers in a Lockheed Hudson. The rump of 258 Squadron still in Singapore and the balance of 232 Squadron were hectically busy over the next few days and suffered serious losses. Meanwhile the Japanese had begun to shell the island

and all remaining aircraft and pilots withdrew to Kallang Airport, the only airfield now out of shelling range. On 10 February all serviceable Hurricanes withdrew to Sumatra while pilots without machines either followed by Lockheed Hudson or were taken to Java by boat.

258 Squadron was one of three squadrons (the others being 242 and 605) which had been originally intended to fly off HMS *Ark Royal* from a point in the Mediterranean to Malta and thence Alexandria. All the pilots of 242 and half of those of 605 had flown off *Ark Royal* but when she was torpedoed and sunk on her return journey the balance were marooned in Gibraltar. When the Far East war broke out the 258 pilots were flown across Africa and boarded *Indomitable* at Port Sudan together with twenty-four pilots of 232 Squadron consisting of the original eighteen, three of 605 and three spare pilots picked up *en route*. Meanwhile, the ground staffs of 242, 258 and 605 Squadrons sailing to the Middle East, were diverted to the Far East. In Sumatra, while 232 Squadron had its own ground crew which had been shipped from Singapore to Palembang,

258 Squadron pilots on flight deck of *Indomitable*
(Author left end front row).

arriving there on 4 February, 258 Squadron was serviced by ground crews who had also been operating in Singapore and were not well experienced on Hurricanes.

So far as bombers were concerned the RAF supplied Blenheims of 84 Squadron which had been re-equipped after service in the Middle East and additional pilots from one or two other squadrons who ferried out reinforcement Blenheims and Hudsons from such places as Heliopolis while the Royal Australian Air Force supplied Lockheed Hudsons of Nos 1 and 8 RAAF Squadrons. These pilots operated from P.2.

Apart from a small force of Dutch-officered native Ambonese or Achinese troops, the only other combatants known to have engaged the Japanese were the personnel of the 12th Battery 6th Regiment Heavy Anti Aircraft with 3.7 guns who had been transferred from Singapore some two or three weeks before the island fell and were stationed at the Pladjoe oil refineries (four guns), at P.1 (eight guns) and P.2 (four guns) and a Dutch Bofors Battery with four guns at each of Pladjoe and P.2 and six at P.1.

As we have seen the Japanese invasion of Sumatra, planned early in January, was to be carried out by the Japanese 38th

Air Vice-Marshal S.F. Vincent CB DFC AFC DL (as Air Commodore).

Division supported by various additional units and spear-headed by paratroops whose numbers alone were greater than the ill-prepared and ill-equipped forces available for the defence of Pladjoe and P.1. Even these small forces occupied their positions almost, as it were, by accident; they were certainly not there as the result of some master plan carefully devised to frustrate the enemy from seizing the invaluable resources and strategic bases of Sumatra.

Early in January of 1942 Air Commodore S.F.Vincent was instructed to proceed to Singapore to command a theoretical Fighter Group of eight squadrons but on reporting to Air Vice-Marshal Pulford was informed by Pulford that no one had told him anything about this and that there simply wasn't a job for him to do. However on 1 February (by which time the Japanese advance down Malaya had brought them into shelling range of most of Singapore's airfields) Vincent was instructed to form a new Fighter Group, No 226, based on Palembang out of the fighter pilots evacuated from Singapore and the ground staffs best available. It is convenient to take this date, 1 February, as representing that on which an attempt to defend the Palembang area was put together.

The History of No. 226 Group (an official Air Ministry document) gives a clear picture of the state of muddle, shortcomings and unpreparedness at the time when the Japanese High Command was giving the final polish to the invasion plans and the final instructions to its Commanders:

"On February 2nd, approximately forty Hurricane aircraft arrived at P.1 Aerodrome . . . with 232 and 258 Squadrons. In addition a number of Buffalos from other squadrons arrived, but owing to unserviceability and age no use was made of these aircraft and as far as possible they were sent on to Java. No 232 Squadron was commanded by Squadron Leader Llewellyn and 258 Squadron by Squadron Leader Thomson.

"Accommodation at P.1 Aerodrome was non-existent. There were no cooking facilities, dispersal huts, water or heavy A.A., very few slit trenches and the defence consisted of four Dutch Bofors guns and a handful of Dutch ground troops.

"Arrangements were immediately made to provide accom-

The building on a tributary of the River Moesi which had been a brothel and which (with the ladies removed) became the billets of the 258 Squadron pilots.

modation in Palembang where the airmen were billeted on floors of schools or godowns, and makeshift arrangements were made for cooking food. The majority of the men were without equipment as most of their kit had been left in Singapore.

"There was a complete lack of transport. The position improved slightly later but there were substantial deficiencies throughout operations both in Sumatra and Java. Not only was it extremely difficult to find sufficient transport for conveying ground personnel to the aerodromes, but there were no vehicles for use of defence personnel so that the sections were unable to move rapidly in the event of attack. This seriously affected the defence of P.1 Aerodrome when later attacked by parachute troops.

"The Dutch had a small operations room in Palembang with a single and bad telephone line to the aerodrome connected with the duty pilot. No lines were available to dispersal points. This position was not and could not be remedied owing to lack of equipment. R/T to aircraft was most unsatisfactory. The transmitter was in the Navy building some considerable distance away and any transmissions had to be sent over the telephone to this building and then transmitted by someone else – in some cases a Dutchman – who was quite unaccustomed to this work. The receiver consisted of a small private wireless set in the operations room. This set was much influenced by the daily heavy electrical storms. The Ops. table consisted merely of a 1:500,000 map with a small number of Observer Corps posts marked on it, and there was no means of plotting enemy or friendly aircraft or any other information.

"The Observer Corps consisted of a number of posts arranged in two concentric circles round Palembang, one at 50 kilometres radius and one at 100 kilometres radius. In addition there were a few posts further out – one at the North end of Banka Island, one at the mouth of the Moesi River and one at Tanjong Pinang Island just south of Singapore. These last two were of great assistance, but the other posts were comparatively thinly manned, aircraft recognition was virtually non-existent and in general the warning was given from the 50 kilometre posts. This gave very little time to sound the alarm and to get the fighters in the air. Communication between the posts and centre was either by W/T operated by locally trained natives or by means of tapping telephone wires . . .

"There was no R/D/F (Radio Direction Finding) and no D/F (Direction Finding) for homing aircraft in bad weather. This deficiency was a serious handicap, particularly in view of the daily tropical storms which made flying extremely unpleasant and homing very difficult.

"Hurricane tool kits were almost non-existent and it was necessary to service aircraft with any tools which could be locally purchased or made. Aircraft spares were similarly almost non-existent and supplies of ammunition, particularly A.P. (armour piercing) and de Wilde (incendiary) were extremely low, as were glycol (cooling fluid) and oxygen supplies. There were no battery charging facilities at the aerodrome and no battery starters for the aircraft. 258 Squadron aircraft were serviced by Buffalo ground crews and all these factors contributed to a low state of serviceability . . .

"Arrangements were made to impound transport and to improve accommodation and feeding arrangements, and for receiving the ground personnel of three squadrons who were expected to arrive shortly from Batavia.

"R/T communications were improved by connecting to the transmitter in the Navy building by direct line to the controller in the Ops. Room, and all personnel who could be spared were ordered to dig slit trenches at the aerodrome.

"The majority of ground personnel were unarmed, the total number of rifles and revolvers held by all RAF personnel in the whole of Sumatra being two or three hundred.

"It was considered that eight Browning guns per Hurricane were sufficient for the unarmoured Japanese aircraft, and that the removal of four from the twelve-gun aircraft would give additional manœuvrability and more rapid climbing. The four outside Brownings were therefore removed and 50 per cent of these were used for spares and 50 per cent for ground defence. Arrangements were made with a local firm to make ground mountings for these guns, but unfortunately the attack on the aerodrome took place before the mountings were completed."

Thus was the stage set: on the one hand a massive fully instructed invasion force of war-hardened men gathering at Camranh Bay, nearly five hundred paratroopers already in final training for their exercise, very substantial allocations of fighter and bomber aircraft, of transports and naval ships, of equipment and supplies all made; and, on the other hand, perhaps two dozen fully serviceable Hurricanes some of whose pilots had yet to have battle experience, perhaps fifty more or less serviceable Blenheim and Hudson bombers at P.2, a Bofors battery and an anti-aircraft battery (as yet without ammunition) split between three locations, and a weak, motley collection of ground forces plagued with communication and language problems and, apart from the native troops, largely unarmed, feverishly trying to create some sort of organization. The odds were hardly favourable.

It may well be assumed that with the fate of Singapore in the balance, the higher echelons of Allied command had little or no knowledge of the situation at Palembang. This was not entirely so. It happened that Wavell *en route* to Australia landed at P.1 in, as I recall, a Flying Fortress, and presumably only for the purpose of refuelling. Amongst the pilots of 258 Squadron on readiness was one of our five Americans, Pilot Officer Kleckner – 'Kleck' as we called him. Kleckner was a husky Texan who was not in the least overawed and pre-empting any higher ranking officers hastily polishing their buttons, he strode out and met the General half-way between his aircraft and the terminal building. And there they stood for the time it took for refuelling to be completed – perhaps twenty minutes – chatting. And the subject of their conversation, as Kleckner was to relay to us once Wavell was on his way, was the situation at P.1, our problems and our shortages. And for good measure Kleckner had thrown in his own opinions as to why it had all gone wrong so far and what should be done to make sure it didn't go so wrong in future. I have often wondered what Wavell thought of Kleckner's views. But Kleck couldn't have given it much more thought – he was shot down and killed very shortly afterwards.

Pilot Officer Cardell Kleckner, one of the five American pilots in 258 Squadron.

The Sumatran Campaign opened with air attacks on P.1. Both the Japanese Monograph No 69 and the *History of 226 Group* give the date of the first raid as 6 February – a date which does not tally with entries in my log-book made at the time. Nor do the Monograph and the History agree on detail. The Monographs state that on 6 February Palembang was attacked by a force consisting of one reconnaissance plane and thirty-two fighters, that the attack took place at 1730 hours, that sixty Allied aircraft were seen to be on the ground of which eleven were destroyed together with a further fifteen which were shot down in combat. A bombing force of thirty-three bombers was also to take part but because of poor weather conditions at the time their objective was changed to Muntok.

The parallel account in the History reads:

"6.2.42. At about 1100 hours the first attack was made on P.1 Aerodrome by bombers and fighters. The warning given by the Observer Corps arrived minutes only before the enemy air-craft, so that the Hurricanes were unable to gain height in time and were attacked in ones and twos immediately after taking off. There was no reasonable R/T communication. Due to these factors and the inexperience of the pilots, four Hurricanes were lost and only one Navy '0' fighter, probably destroyed, with one or two possibly damaged. Subsequently, three of the Hurricane pilots – one injured – returned."

This account is so utterly at variance with what I still recall, and the very full version I wrote within a short time of the occasion, that it surely must refer to quite another raid. My own account was written many years ago and was based on detailed notes taken at the time and I have since discovered no new facts which incline me to change it, nor have any of the surviving pilots with whom I shared those hectic days, most of whom have read the account, suggested it is in error. Indeed their own accounts largely confirm it:

"The flight from Singapore on February 3rd had been made in the early morning and in the afternoon, as was the rule, it rained in torrents. Later the rain abated but for a while the sky remained entirely covered by heavy threatening cloud with only a small break to the north. We, the pilots, sat in a line on chairs on the verandah in front of the terminal building facing the end of the north-south runway chatting and smoking. The readiness state, that is to say the list of pilots on duty to fly that afternoon, was chalked on the glass. I was not listed having been on readiness through the morning, there being insufficient serviceable aircraft for more than about every other pilot to be able to fly.

"I suppose as we sat there watching the steam rising from the runways as they dried in the stifling, heavy heat we were thinking, and talking, about doomed Singapore from which we had just by the skin of our teeth escaped, and the fortuitous fact that with all that was going on around us we were still unharmed. I suppose, too, we were conscious that we represented the approximate total defence, apart from a handful of native troops, of an island of which we might well never have heard before but which turned out to be large enough into which to drop the whole of Italy and leave plenty of room all round. And I suppose we were talking about how it would be after a few days to get ourselves organized and when the expected reinforcements of Hurricanes, still in Java, had arrived.

"Whatever it might have been, it was to the last subject that conversation switched when we heard the note of aircraft engines. There were sounds of satisfaction; some of those in their chairs stood and strolled out to the airfield, others again, including me, decided it was too hot, too hot and too sticky, and stayed where we were.

"I remember being quite impressed that with miles of cloud above, the Hurricanes had found P.1 and thinking how lucky it was there was that one break or they could never have landed and might have been very pushed to make it back to Java. And it was then that we saw the first of the Hurricanes break into view in the small blue gap to the north in the mass of sullen cloud like overlapping slates which otherwise roofed the sky. Only, of course, it wasn't a Hurricane but a Navy 0. We watched the first and then, one by one, the others, still tiny specks, lazing pouring through the gap diving on us in the traditional beat up. It was the expected thing on arriving at a new station, to beat it up. It told everyone you were arriving; it made everyone stop whatever they were doing to look at you; it brought people inside buildings outside or at least to the window; it drowned all conversation.

"It was only when the fighters were comparatively near we realized they had radial engines, that they weren't Hurricanes. It took only moments to realize what they were – Navy 0's. And by then it was too late! The air was filled with the whine of bullets and cannon shells and the roar of engines. The first Navy Nought pulled out of its dive and climbed away from its first attack not twenty feet above my head, the blood red circles on its wings mocking us. Behind me was the sound of shattering glass and yards to my left a man was screaming and clutching at his stomach. The second Navy 0 was already into its attack seeming to be aiming directly at me and not a hundred yards away, its machine guns and cannon blazing. I dropped, and, as it pulled up, ran.

"P.1 was filled with running men: pilots on readiness running to their aircraft, ground staff running out to help them in and start them up, others, with no purpose in remaining, running for the jungle.

"I began to run – and then I had to stop, if briefly, because a few yards away I saw something which seemed to me quite

Pilot Officer J.A. ('Red') Campbell, another of the Americans.

incredible. 'Red' Campbell (one of 258's five American pilots) was standing calmly, revolver in hand, aiming at the next Navy 0. it was useless of course, but not a gesture. One does read of men who have no fear but they are very rare. Campbell was one of them.

"There is something very different about being a helpless recipient of general bombing such as a city's inhabitants have to endure and being the specific target. While the danger in the latter is obviously much greater, there is much more to occupy one's mind than simply crossing one's fingers, waiting and hoping for the best. And there was certainly a lot of drama in that first blooding of this particular kind of warfare.

"There were one's friends taxiing past at dangerous speeds and tearing down the runway to do battle; there were the strafing Navy 0's; the shriek of aircraft, the shattering of glass, the spatter of machine guns, the pop of cannon and now the slow cudumph, cudumph, cudumph of the Bofors guns. Then there was the added heartening chatter of Brownings. There were air battles to witness against the background of the heavy cloud, a Navy 0 hurtling earthwards in a screaming dive into the jungle, a Hurricane eluding a Japanese which had been sitting on its tail apparently pumping bullets into it, another hit and showing the thin white thread of leaking glycol thicken, yet managing to land. And there was Campbell, nerveless, reloading his revolver.

"When the fraças had died down I went back to the verandah and picking up my chair, which had fallen over, saw there was a neat bullet hole through one of its chromium legs. I went into the terminal building and there was damage everywhere and the readiness situation chalked on the glass was in pieces on the floor. I tried to make a jigsaw to find out who was flying. The Bofors guns had fallen silent and the sky was fast clearing of clouds. I went out again and now there were no aircraft to be seen, only the more distant sounds of them and men were fast emerging from the jungle.

"Although I do not remember this there was an ironical result from the strafing which might have made the Japanese smile had they been aware of it. Apparently (I had this from Thomson – Commanding Officer of 258 Squadron), there was a splendid picture of a line of British battleships, white ensigns proudly flying, hung on a wall of the terminal building. By the time the Navy 0s had finished with us, this impressive piece of propaganda was hanging at a drunken angle threatening to hit the floor at any instant. This would not have mattered all that much but for its caption: 'The downfall of the dictators is assured.'

"Curiously the attack had been an almost total failure. Of the aircraft which managed to get airborne all landed safely – mostly at P.2. A few ground staff personnel were killed and wounded.

"None of the aircraft on the ground were damaged."

The *History of 226 Group* account is so much at variance with both the Japanese version and my own, that it must, surely, refer to another raid. The time of day is wrong; the casualties are wrong; above all the reference to a warning is wrong – had there been a warning, we would hardly have been sitting

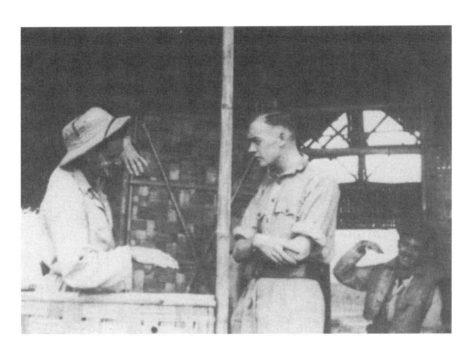

Author in dispersal shelter listening doubtfully to another pilot's explanation of how he achieved a kill!

around chatting and smoking! Moreover, when we come to the next attack, which I have noted as taking place on 4 February and the History (and, admittedly, the Japanese Monograph) records as being on 7 February, there is again only limited similarity.

According to the Monographs, the Japanese, believing that approximately thirty Allied aircraft still remained at P.1, carried out a further attack on the following day by six bombers and thirty-one fighters drawn from units of the 59th, 64th and 90th Air Regiments at 1520 hours in which twenty planes were destroyed on the ground and ten engaged in the air of which the majority were shot down for the loss of two Japanese aircraft.

The History reads:
"7.2.42. The Japanese again raided P.1 with bombers and low flying fighters, and a large number of aircraft was destroyed on the ground. Once again the warning came late . . . Six Blenheims and three Hurricanes were totally burnt out and approximately eleven more Hurricanes damaged together with one Buffalo and one Hudson which had just landed. In the air three Hurricanes were shot down – two pilots returning later. One probable Navy '0' was claimed with one or two damaged. In addition one Blenheim which was just coming in to land at the time of the raid was shot down and the pilot killed."

My own account reads:
"We were not always so fortunate and, in fact, one of the worst days of all was the next, February 4th, when the airfield was again attacked in a raid much better planned. This time there were bombers and the Japanese did not make the error of having their whole force strafe in a combined attack. Again there was no warning and this time there were fighters waiting to pick off the Hurricanes waiting to do battle with them.
"We flew several times that day and by the end of it nine 258 Squadron aircraft were missing or shot down and others damaged and in fact out of the entire force the only two Hurricanes which managed to get back to P.1 undamaged were my own and Bertie Lambert's. Three 258 Squadron pilots were

Hurricane of 258 Squadron on readiness. Note absence of squadron letters owing to insufficient time to have these painted.

dead, one was dying, two were missing and three had been badly shot about and their pilots either baled out or crash landed in swamp or on airfield."

So far as the following day is concerned the Japanese Monographs state that a further raid was made by seventeen bombers and twenty-five fighters from units of 59th, 64th and 90th Air Regiments in which two Allied planes were shot down and nine destroyed and in a second raid of seven bombers and twenty-nine fighters of the 59th, 64th, 75th and 90th Air Regiments, five planes were shot down and four destroyed for the loss of three Japanese planes.

On 8 February, I flew down with other pilots in a Lockheed Loadstar to Java to ferry up more Hurricanes and so have no notes of any action on that day. According to the 226 Group History, P.1 was again attacked but this time there was more warning and the Hurricane pilots were able to climb to a sufficient height before the Japanese arrived and intercepted them. The History adds that the raid was of very short duration and no definite casualties were caused to either side. On the other hand the Operational Record Book of 232 Squadron, one of the squadrons in 226 Group, not only records that two of the squadron pilots were lost but gives their names (Flt Lt E.M.Taylor and Sgt Pilot S.M.Hackforth), the numbers of the aircraft they were flying and details of how they were shot down – Taylor while circling P.1 and Hackforth after being attacked by five Navy 0s. This Operational Record Book was, again, prepared well after these events took place (in fact at the end of March by the Squadron Adjutant 'from his own personal notebook' with assistance from two 232 pilots who had been evacuated following injury). So far as my own summary of losses to 258 Squadron in the period is concerned, I have noted that four pilots, Kleckner, (PO) Scott, Keedwell and Glynn were killed and Nichols, (Sgt) Scott, Nash, White and McCulloch were shot down but survived and these names accord with the numbers of aircraft given by me as shot down over the period.

It is not, of course, of vital importance whether the 226 Group History, the 232 Operational Record Book or my own log-book and other notes are correct; nor does it really matter

Sergeant Pilot Roy Keedwell, one of the two Canadians. He died of burns after crash-landing following action near Palembang.

whether these three raids took place on 3, 4 and 5 or 6, 7 and 8 February. What does matter is that they were carried out by the Japanese with the express intention of wiping out all fighter opposition before the invasion of Sumatra took place. They failed in this objective although they certainly much reduced the opposition they might otherwise have met.

The main cause of their failure was of course the existence of P.2. It seems remarkable that an airfield of such enormous size, in flying terms so near to P.1, should have remained un-detected. Admittedly being devoid of the usual buildings the Japanese had come to expect to find on captured Allied airfields, it did appear from the air to be no more than a vast jungle clearing; admittedly it was possible largely to conceal aircraft not actually taking off or landing under the shield of trees on the perimeter. But even taking these factors into account it was astonishing it was not discovered, the more so as the Japanese had more or less accepted there must be an alternative airfield from which Hurricanes, all of which had reputedly been destroyed in the previous day's attack, emerged.

A further factor which would have added to the confusion in the minds of the Japanese was the construction of imitation aircraft which were left littered around P.1. Strafing is a very exciting operation carried out at great speed and at such low levels that ground is covered at quite terrifying pace. The dive is begun distantly from the airfield and the objects to be attacked picked out when they are tiny. When the gun button is fired, adrenalin is flowing swiftly while the mind is fully occupied with both keeping the aircraft nose-down in line with the target and judging when to pull out and avoid collison with obstacles on the field's perimeter. There simply is not time when passing over cleverly constructed dummy aircraft to appreciate that they are fakes.

The above two points are perhaps best illustrated by referring again to the Japanese records of the results of their three consecutive days attack on P.1. On the first day, it will be recalled, they claimed to have strafed sixty planes on the ground, on the second twenty and on the third to have more or less completed the destruction of the enemy air force. They were to discover, bloodily, this was not the case.

We must now turn our attention to P.2 itself to see what was happening there. The conditions are aptly described by Group Captain (at the time Flt Lt) H.C.Plenty, a Lockheed Hudson pilot of No 8 Squadron RAAF.

"One's chief impression of P.2. was of an organized state of chaos. Distances between living quarters, ops room and dispersals were some three miles and up to two miles respectively. Victualling was rather spartan; for the first couple of weeks the only meat available was zebu, rather strong, stringy and monotonous. There was practically no motor transport: crews had to hike most times between quarters, ops room and dispersal. Group HQ often issued orders requiring crews to flit between these points in unattainable times. Even Sebastian Coe could not have done so on foot . . . Most refuelling was done from 40-gallon drums. Bombs were manhandled into bomb bays. And, Jesus, the climate was HOT."

Plenty's squadron began operations from P.2 on 6 February; the sister Australian squadron, No 1 Squadron, had become operational one week earlier. The official RAAF History compiled by W.R.Lyster gives details of the operations of the two squadrons which for the period prior to the invasion read:

"No 1 Squadron recommenced operations on 31 January by sending five aircraft to attack the enemy occupied aerodrome of Alor Star in northern Malaya . . . Before reaching the Malayan coast they encountered very bad weather and the formation broke up. Two aircraft still kept company and the other three attacked individually. Between 0430 and 0450 they were over the target in sequence. As the attacks were from an average height of five thousand feet the crews were able to see the hits on the metal runway, the hangars and the administrative buildings. There was no enemy air activity and no A/A and all our aircraft returned safely.

"On 1 and 2 February No 1 Squadron carried out reconnaissance sweeps of the South Java Sea and of the south China Sea in search of enemy surface vessels and submarines, and returned on both days with a nil sighting report. On the same day, February 2nd, three aircraft of No 1 Squadron took off . . . to make an attack on Singgora . . . One Hudson was forced to return with engine trouble; the other two proceeded to

Singgora . . . from where there had been a report of heavy concentration of rolling stock and war material. Both pilots straddled the target with their sticks of bombs at 0400 hours on February 3 . . . and returned to P.2.

"On 3, 4 and 5 February No 1 Squadron continued its reconnaissance of the waters around Sumatra and of the South China Sea to gain early information of any Japanese preparations for the invasion of Java or Sumatra, but reported no movements except those of our own ships proceeding south from Singapore. One pilot reported seeing several ships on fire in the islands south of Singapore on 4 February.

"On 5 February two Hudsons of No 1 Squadron took off for Seletar in company with 11 Hurricanes (which would have been of 232 Squadron) and on arrival there were forced to proceed, by Japanese artillery, successively to Sembawang, to Tengah and finally to Kallang. The captains of the aircraft who were Flt. Lts. J.G.Emerton and J.A.Lockwood, had instructions to bring out the A.O.C. (Air Vice-Marshal Pulford) and other senior RAF officers. The Hudsons returned to P.2 with various passengers, though the A.O.C. chose to remain . . . (accompanied by) the four remaining Buffalos of 453 Squadron.

"No 8 Squadron . . . were ready for flying by 5 February. On that day two aircraft, flown by R.A.F. crews attached to No. 8 Squadron, did a reconnaissance of the South China Sea for any hostile enemy convoy, but returned with a negative sighting . . .

"Intelligence reports about 5 February stated that an enemy airborne attack on Palembang was likely and in consequence immediate measures were taken to defend P.2 and its approaches . . .

"About this time a Japanese cypher message was intercepted and decoded, indicating that an enemy convoy was assembling in the Anambas Islands. No 1 Squadron was detailed for a reconnaissance and left P.2 at 0620 hours on 6 February. As there was no cloud cover *en route* the first pilot, Flg. Off. P.J.Gibbes, climbed to 15,000 feet and over the Anambas Islands found 7/10 cloud at 2,000 feet. At Metak in the Anambas group seven fighters were seen at 5,000 feet climbing in a southerly direction towards the Hudson, and almost immediately three fighters were seen at 12,000 feet coming in from the port quarter – all believed to be Navy '0's. The Hudson took evasive action by diving into cumulus cloud 5,000 feet below. It was impossible to reconnoitre north of Latitude 03 deg. 20' N. in the group but the second pilot, Flg. Off. A.B. Jay drew a good sketch of Metak Bay and the ships therein which were: one cruiser (Kako Class), four destroyers and four merchant ships of about 10,000, 5,000 and 3,000 tons respectively. The ships were at anchor . . .

"Enemy fighters continued to attack for about forty-five miles but evasive tactics continued to be successful and the Hudson sustained no damage . . .

"As a result of this report an attack was ordered on the Anambas Islands. Ten Blenheim Mk. IV's were to have been accompanied by five Hudsons from 8 Squadron but after working out the distance to be covered with a full bomb load, and considering the range of the Hudsons, it was decided to leave them out. Another factor was the extreme difficulty in locating P.2 after dark.

"Routine reconnaissance of the South China Sea continued each day. Their task was both to give warning of Japanese invasion and also to sweep ahead of Allied convoys proceeding out of Singapore. These recces of the South China Sea continued to have negative results until February 13 when reports of Japanese convoys to the north of Banka Island were brought in. No 1 Squadron diary comments in the following fashion upon the searches carried out on the 13th. 'For some reason best known to themselves Group H.Q. did not order for this day the usual reconnaissance of four or five Hudsons to sweep the South China Sea which might have avoided the confusion and lack of appreciation of the situation which arose later in the day. A definite report from a properly planned search would have revealed the true situation and been of enormous value to aircraft which proceeded on bombing on the following day. As it happened on this day aircraft were only sent out at odd intervals to confirm reports of some other origin of convoys in the vicinity of the north of Banka Island. Each aircraft that went out reported a Japanese convoy in different strength and different positions.' One of these aircraft so detailed was from No 1 Squadron and its report was inconclusive as it was intercepted and forced to take evasive action. These Japanese fighters were presumed to come off a carrier. Two other sightings were brought in by No 8 Squadron aircraft.

"Apart from reconnaissance work the RAAF Hudsons continued to be employed on special missions and upon the bombing of enemy aerodromes. On February 10 two aircraft of No 1 Squadron, captains being Flt. Lts. K.R.Smith and C.C.Verco, took off at 0300 hours to bring out the A.O.C. from Singapore. This was a particularly dangerous period to attempt to land since the air was filled with fighters and dive bombers and the shelling of the three northern aerodromes was intense. However, under cover of a dense pall of smoke from the burning oil tanks at the naval base, the aircraft reached Kallang just before dawn. As the A.O.C. was not prepared to leave Singapore, Air Commodore Staton and other senior RAF officers were carried instead to P.2. On arrival Air Commodore Staton requested that another aircraft be sent to Singapore for the A.O.C., even though the chance of getting through in daylight hours was slight. Flt. Lt. Smith with the same crew took off on their second trip at 1030 hours and this time returned with Air Vice-Marshal Maltby and others, though the A.O.C. Air Vice-Marshal Pulford, still chose to remain in Singapore."

Ambitious plans were laid for 12 February but it proved to be a frustrating day. Twenty-three Blenheims were to attack shipping in the Anambas Islands while eleven Hudsons were to bomb Kluang airfield. The first batch of Blenheims started taking off in the very early hours but two of them crashed in the trees near No 1 Squadron's dispersal pens, another in attempting to land again hit a building while a fourth did get down but was badly damaged in the process – taking off and landing from P.2, particularly at night, was a somewhat hazardous operation and there was much criticism that the flare path was too short or wrongly laid out; Group Captain Plenty comments that the Hudson pilots used to switch on their landing lights while taking off and he vividly recalls how he saw the trees illuminated ahead of him as he lifted off and how, by setting the maximum angle of climb, he managed to scrape over them. After these crashes the bombs of the first two Blenheims

Flight Lieutenant (later Group Captain) H.C. Plenty, one of the Australian bomber pilots.

started exploding putting No 1 Squadron's aircraft at serious risk and the Squadron Commander had them led down the field with the aid of headlights to the take-off point; meanwhile instructions were given to the Blenheim crews, who were by now in a somewhat confused state of mind, to abort their mission.

At 0215 hours the eleven Hudsons started taking off and this having been achieved by them all without a hitch, they set off for and bombed Kluang where they were met by dense anti-aircraft fire and, for the first time, by night fighters. However they suffered no casualties and having observed hits on the airfield, its hangars and its buildings, returned safely to P.2.

3

Exodus from Singapore

By now the exodus from Singapore was in full flood as was well described by Lionel Wigmore in his book *The Japanese Thrust* published in Australia in 1957. He told of how the seas between Singapore, Sumatra and Java were, for several days, dotted with small craft seeking to run the gauntlet of Japanese sea and air forces; of a state of utter confusion; of how of the one hundred men officially required to be got away from Singapore by the Australian authorities, only thirty-nine succeeded; of Major-General Gordon Bennett, Commanding Officer of the 8th Australian Division in Singapore who, unlike Pulford, did not hesitate to quit the island, and, together with a Major Moses, a Lieutenant Walker and some planters who had been serving as volunteers in Malaya, took charge of a native craft and made an adventurous trip to the east coast of Sumatra, crossed Sumatra to Padang, from Padang to Java, and from Java to Australia, reaching Melbourne on 2 March. After the war there was an enquiry, with a somewhat inconclusive result, into the circumstances connected with the action of General Bennett relinquishing his command and leaving Singapore. I have had many opinions given to me about Bennett, mostly very uncomplimentary, from Australians who have helped me with this book, but perhaps the most damning words of all are those from Bennett's own lips when reporting on the call he made on General Sturdee, then chief of the Australian General Staff, immediately following his escape: 'To my dismay, my reception was cold and hostile. No other member of the Military Board called to see me. After a few minutes formal conversation, Sturdee told me my escape was ill-advised, or

Conference prior to the signing of surrender by the Japanese in south-east Asia. Left to right: Admiral Jin-Icha Kusaka (CIC Japanese south-east Navy), General Imamura (CIC Japanese far-east Army), Lieutenant General V.A.H.Sturdee (GOC 1st Australian Army), Brigadier E.L.Sheehan, BGS and Captain Wass Buzzard.

words to that effect . . . He then went on with his work, leaving me to stand aside in his room.'

Air Commodore Modin, who was to be the Senior British Officer in the prison camp in Palembang and after the war Secretary of the RAF Yacht Club, gives his own account of the situation in the seas to the south of Singapore: 'The enemy appeared to have achieved complete surprise in closing the Banka Strait just when the final and heaviest flow of evacuation craft from Singapore might be expected to pass. It would seem that few, if any, intelligence reports, or warnings, of enemy activity, in or above the Banka Strait were received by our vessels and I doubt whether the capture of so many surface craft has ever been achieved with greater ease.'

There are any number of individual stories which could be

recounted of the experiences of the thousands of civilian men, women and children and of servicemen now desperately trying to escape from the Japanese – some of courage, some of imagination and resource, some of great personal sacrifice. And it must be remembered that just as those who were shortly to be involved in defending P.1 against the Japanese had not the least idea that this mass evacuation from Singapore was taking place, so were those involved in this evacuation either as escapers or as rescuers, quite ignorant of the situation obtaining a mere two hundred miles to the south of them.

There were, it seems, two officers who in Lionel Wigmore's words: 'became principally active in organising aid for the participants in the strange migration'. These were Captain I. Lyon of the Gordon Highlanders and Major H.A.Campbell of the King's Own Scottish Borderers. Captain Lyon 'assisted by an RAMC private, established a dump of food and shelter on an uninhabited part of an island near Moro, in the south western part of the Rhio Archipelago. Here, until the evening of February 17th, first aid and sailing directions were given and rations were provided for the next stage of the journey.' Major Campbell 'had arranged with the Dutch authorities in Sumatra means whereby transport, food and clothing were provided.' Campbell organized the principal escape route used, that up the Inderagiri River to Rengat and thence by road to the railhead of Sawahlunto and from here to Padang. 'Instructions about the route and navigation of the Inderagiri were supplied at Priggi Rajah at the mouth of the river. At Tambilahan a surgical hospital was set up and further aid was given. Escapers were rested and regrouped into suitable parties at Rengat, and at Ayer Molek near by . . . A British military headquarters was set up at Padang to handle evacuations and help the Dutch defend the town if necessary.'

It all sounds very efficient and one cannot but reflect that it was a pity the same efficiency being displayed in getting men away from the Japanese was not being displayed in resisting them. Moreover, even if the majority of the escapers had no idea of what was going on at Palembang to the south, it is highly improbable that those running the affair at Rengat did not, for there would have been telephonic communication between the towns. Moreover there was a road (an easier and shorter road than that between Rengat and Padang) between Rengat and Pakanbaroe where there was another airfield which was being supplied from P.2. It is ironical that, had some of those being organized to escape instead been airlifted to P.1, the airfield might have held against the paratroops.

Friday the thirteenth of February, nineteen hundred and forty-two, was for many to justify superstition. On Singapore chaos and confusion reigned. The Japanese generals, astonished by the paucity of the resistance offered by an enemy which so outnumbered them, were preparing the surrender documents; General Percival, who had already accepted the inevitability of defeat, cabled Wavell that the Japanese were within five thousand yards of the sea-front and that his troops were too exhausted either to withstand a strong attack or to launch a counter-attack. Without putting this in specific terms he sought approval to capitulate. Wavell rejected the plea but this was merely window-dressing – his message to Churchill on the following day advised that resistance was now unlikely to be prolonged.

In accordance with a prepared scheme for evacuating key personnel from Singapore a huge stream of nominated evacuees, their numbers swelled by many deserters, descended on the docks and harbour areas and hastily boarded (in some cases forcing those already in possession to accept their company at gunpoint) all manner of small craft: launches, junks, sampans, rowboats, fishing trawlers. Anything which would float was pressed into service, commandeered or simply stolen. Ahead, as we have seen, lay an open sea totally controlled by the Japanese Navy and Air Force; behind, under a pall of smoke from burning oil stores and installations, the doomed, defeated island.

Amongst the men whose services were considered too valuable for them to be left to be taken prisoner were two men, both regular soldiers (one of whom would succeed in escaping and one of whom would fail) whose experiences were to be very typical of the great majority of those who set out on this largely forlorn and desperate exercise. The first of these was Major Donald Wright who had been on the staff of the Third Indian

Corps and the other was Brigadier Bird who was on Headquarters Staff of Fortress Command, Singapore, as an
instructor in gunnery.

Both men left Singapore in different craft; Wright on a small
motor boat, the *Hung Jow*, which accommodated thirteen
evacuees and Bird on a narrow, high-speed motor launch, some
one hundred feet in length, which took about eighty men.
Casting off under cover of darkness they slowly made their way,
passing close by the burning liner *Empress of Asia* which, having
run aground after bombing, was burning fiercely and, together
with the inferno of blazing Singapore itself, was lighting up the
armada of fleeing boats and exposing them to constant shelling.
But these men's hopes were high – on the island there were the
two alternatives, death or imprisonment, but southwards,
within little more than twenty-four hours' sailing, as yet, so far
as they knew, unscathed, lay Sumatra and freedom. They
had, like the sixty-five nurses on the *Vyner Brooke*, the eighty
men commanded by Lt Wilkinson on the *Li Wo* and Captain
Carston, captain of the *Mata Hari*, with almost five hundred
refugees, men, women and children aboard, who had all left
Singapore the previous day, no idea that a massive Japanese
fleet covering the Sumatran invasion force lay athwart their
path.

Meanwhile, on instructions from Wavell, the Dutch Admiral
Doorman was assembling on the south coast of Java the
balance of the naval forces remaining to the ABDA Command
preparatory to sailing northwards to the Banka Strait to
intercept the enemy fleet. Doorman had at his disposal one
heavy cruiser the British *Exeter*, four light cruisers, the
Australian *Hobart* and the Dutch *De Ruyter*, *Tromp* and *Java* and
ten destroyers, a substantial force in its own right but a modest
one compared with that of the Japanese whose combined
Southern Expeditionary Fleet commanded by Vice-Admiral
Ozawa and two echelons under Rear-Admiral Hashimoto and
Captain Kojima respectively, mustered an aircraft-carrier, six
heavy cruisers, eleven destroyers and various other vessels.

Thus the extraordinary situation obtained that a totally
unprotected armada of mainly tiny craft was, under official
instructions, (referred to by Churchill as a 'prepared scheme
for evacuating to Java by sea some three thousand nominated

individuals') setting out to thread its way through the maze of islands, large and small, which, straddling the Equator, lie between Singapore and Sumatra, quite unaware they were heading into a sea bristling with enemy ships whilst at the same time an Allied fleet was, also under official instructions, hastily gathering itself to meet this very circumstance. In a way there was to be to these thousands of men and women, civilian and military, young and old, creaming the blue tropical waters in their launches, bobbing about in their little boats, inching their way through minefields in the darkness, crammed hot and perspiring exposed both to enemy bombing and the cruel, blazing equatorial sun by day, a horrible similarity to a land-based rabble of evacuees heading in blind ignorance into a hoped-for sanctuary which was to prove a battlefield.

We shall return to the plight of these evacuees and their adventures in due course.

4
Prelude to Invasion

While the men and women who had escaped from stricken Singapore were fleeing southwards the ground staffs of the fighter squadrons who had been disembarked in Java were heading northwards. Martin Ofield, of 605 County of Warwickshire Auxiliary Squadron, pithily summarizes their arrival in Sumatra on Sunday 8 February: "Disembarked at Oosthaven. Then by train arriving at a railhead after dark, marching a couple of miles to reach the Moesi River, crossing by ferry and then being taken by trucks to billets. We were divided into two groups. I was with one group taken to a school being constructed and the other group was accommodated about a mile away in a warehouse building. We learnt that we were at Palembang. On the following day we were addressed by a senior officer who brought us up to date with the war situation – we had heard little definite news for weeks. Singapore was expected to fall at any time and the Japanese were likely to attack Palembang, probably using paratroops. We had expected to find our planes and pilots here as they had left England before we did, but there were only two, Wright and Hutton, from whom we gathered we should have gone to the Middle East. Two other squadrons of our wing became operational at P.1 but as there were insufficient aircraft for 605, our unit therefore provided a daytime working party for trench digging and a night-time guard patrol."

Hedley Bonnes, also of 605 Squadron, gives a more graphic description:
    "We landed in Java at Tandjeonpriok and we went up to the

Hedley A. Bonnes.

aerodrome and operated from there for a time servicing aircraft. You know, we nailed a few together that had been knocked about. A couple of Wildebeests we got going, that sort of thing. There were plenty of aircraft about. There were American aircraft still in packing cases. I think they were Buffalos.

"We were then sort of paraded one day and they marched us down to the railway station and put us on a train which took us to the local port from where we boarded a ship which took us to Oosthaven, near Krakatoa. It's the only time in my life (and I never want to hear it again) I heard someone say: 'fall in facing the ship', not 'fall in facing the boat!' We then got on the boat. We sailed a long way and we were not quite used to the tropical heat and this native on board decided to slaughter a bullock and its guts were all over the blooming deck! And we then got across to Oosthaven and were put on another train, which was a wood burning locomotive, and we thundered all the way to Palembang. Took a long time – a day to get there, a day and a half, something like that. I remember getting off the train late at night. We got to Palembang rather late and we had to get off with our kit and we were carrying endless spares and that sort of thing and our personal gear. And we had no transport of course and we were marched down to the river where we waited for some time before we got some sort of boat across. It was a terribly fast flowing river and we went across and we were put in a warehouse. Then our bits and bobs caught up with us, you know, spares and so forth, and we legged it up to the aerodrome the next morning. P.1. Then of course we had to sort ourselves out regarding ground defence and so forth. I know one of the things I was put in charge of . . . I was a fitter armourer, for God's sake, a gunner! They gave me a bloody steamroller to look after! I mean, what are you going to do with a steamroller? You know, in an air raid? You're not going to drive it. So I did the obvious thing: crawled underneath the damn thing. Not a bad place to be. I was better off than another chap. He had a thing with a scoop on the front for earth moving.

"Anyway we got shot up a bit as you know at P.1. and I remember being with Perks and Broadmoor on one occasion, same two blokes who got killed the next day, I think. And we were strafed that day. The only notification we had of aircraft coming over, these Zeros, was the flag going up. By that time they were shooting at us. A red flag on the top!

"It was a bit hectic, you know, but it was a sort of gentlemanly war even at that time because we packed it in when it got dusk and went back to Palembang. I stayed at the aerodrome a couple of times. There was an awful lot to do up there. Slept in the terminal building lying on the floor in an old sleeping bag I had . . ."

Palembang owed its existence to two factors: the oil at Pladjoe and this river, which, and in a way the town, was well described by Tom Jackson of 605 in a diary he kept at the time:

"February 9th 1942. The river was an amazing sight. We stood on the bank and watched it rushing by. It was frightening, dirty and awe-inspiring. It was also full of darned great alligators. Tiny little cockleshell boats were bobbing about in the current, the crews paddling for grim death. It seemed to take them a long time to cover a little distance, but I soon found out that they were fishing and only wanted to keep more or less stationary. We went back to Borsumy (corruption of the

The Moesi River at Palembang.

A 1982 photograph of Palembang.

Borneo Sumatra Trading Company) after a while, walking through the town under our own steam. I bought a block of Rowntree's Chocolate Crisp of which there seemed to be a lot about, a pineapple slice which had been frozen and a bunch of bananas. The street hawkers fascinated me, they seemed to be selling everything there ever was for sale! Bootlaces to a cooked dinner! Iced drinks, 'Gone With The Wind', toothpaste, Yankee magazines, Times Supplements, packets of foreign stamps, fried banana fritters, chops, rice, brown sugar, American and English cigarettes, cigars in all sizes, shoes, umbrellas and topees. Woolworths hadn't a look in. The frozen pineapple was delicious. I always found that fresh pineapple made the sides of my mouth very sore and I didn't eat much of it. I wrote a letter home from Borsumy when I arrived back, and went to bed early under a mosquito net on a brand new mattress."

Quarters for those already at the airfield were described by Martyn Lovejoy, again of 605 Squadron: "Our accommodation was in the jungle at the southern end of the 'drome. The buildings had been taken away from the local inhabitants . . . did I say buildings? That is not true, for in fact they were typical native huts, built off the ground and some going up into the trees. We were not there for more than a couple of days, which was just as well for the lads who had the task of cooking had to put up with the pranks of the local monkeys who pelted them with coconuts whenever they lit a fire. We were convinced they had been trained by the local people whose houses we had stolen. Or perhaps it was they did not like smoke or the smell of cooking. Or did they sense what was to befall us in the hours ahead?"

On P.2 there reigned a calmness rather like that to be found in the eye of a hurricane. The Hudsons and Blenheims, together numbering about fifty, secreted around the edges of this vast, sprawling, jungle airfield, all but invisible under a protecting canopy of foliage, were mute, unused. Their air crews, in the main Australians, lounged around the wooden bungalow which served as mess and crew room, smoking endless cigarettes, bored by inactivity, relieved to be inactive. For several days there had been no flying of consequence. Through the first week of February every aircraft had been pressed into service to carry out night bombing raids over Malaya and daily reconnaissances over the South China Sea but six days before the Japanese invasion fleet arrived to the north of Banka Island, orders had been given that in future reconnaissance would be carried out only from Java to allow a pause for the battle-weary pilots to rest and their aircraft to be repaired and serviced ready to be hurled against the invaders when they came. But the invaders, in convoys totalling more than fifty warships and troop transports, came very near, unobserved, unattacked. The admirals must have been as amazed at the ease of their passage as had been the generals on Singapore at the ease of their advance across the island. Aware they could outrange and outgun any naval force which could be assembled against them, Ozawa and Hashimoto's sole concerns were the possibility of submarine and air attack. Against the former they were well equipped with submarine chasers additional to their many destroyers included with the fleet, but against the latter they were always vulnerable. True, they had the protection of the fighters carried on *Ryujo* and additional cover could be given by aircraft operating from the advanced Malayan bases; but the fearful 'Sumatras' which boiled up every afternoon could provide ideal cloud cover for attacking bombers. No doubt the admirals, appraised of the continuous bombing and strafing of what they firmly believed to be the sole airfield within practicable range for roving bombers and within possible range of the British Hurricanes, P.1, concluded that the squadrons based there had been, for all practical purposes, annihilated. Thus they approached unobserved, unhindered, to within a mere seventy miles of the point where the troops carried on the twenty-eight transports they were escorting would disembark while, barely fifteen minutes' flying time away, forty to fifty Allied bombers stood silent and unused. It was not until the afternoon that a lone Hudson on what has been described as 'local initiative and contrary to restraining orders', carrying out a reconnaissance, spotted the invasion fleet. Even then, only the Blenheims were ordered to attack. This they did in small batches, some of which, because of the appalling weather, failed to locate the target, while the few pilots who did were unable to make any dramatic claims.

If at P.2 there was inertia through the brilliant morning of Friday, 13 February, at P.1 there was drama. With its strength decimated by the continuous activity of the past few days, 258 Squadron were eagerly awaiting reinforcements due to be flown up that day from Java. These consisted of eight Hurricanes led by Wing Commander Maguire and including machines flown by Campbell, (Sergeant) Scott, Milnes and myself.

We took off from Tjillilitan airfield to which we had ferried our aircraft from Kemajoran on the previous day and, flying low, arrived at P.1 two hours later. It has always been my personal recollection that I was flying Number Two to Maguire but his own account of the happenings of that flight seem to contradict this – unless it was that he gave me instructions to land ahead of him which would have been an unusual thing for a Number Two to do. According to Maguire, he was under-carriage down when he was jumped by enemy fighters which had appeared as if from nowhere and had to do a fairly swift manœuvre to get away at, of course, very low level. Chased by a pair of Hayabusas, he could see that the leader was going to turn inside him when, to his astonishment and delight, the Hayabusa's Number Two briskly shot him down and then passing Maguire in the process was himself shot down by Maguire and another Hurricane pilot.

Meanwhile Scott was having troubles of his own. I am quite sure he was the last of the eight of us to land and this is borne out by Campbell's account of what happened to him which closely tallies with my own recollection. Quoted verbatim from the tape he prepared for me, Campbell records:

"Of course we were somewhat short on fuel but as I taxied to the dispersal area and turned round and shut my engine off, I noticed that people were running in all directions and the Hurricanes which were already there were running up and taxiing out madly and I tried to get some fuel and get off again but no one would listen to me, they were all running for the slit trenches. So I figured the smart thing for me to do was to get into a slit trench myself and watch what was going on.

"Meantime Scotty was in the circuit with his wheels and

Sergeant Pilot N.M. Scott. Photograph taken in Burma after he had received his commission.

(*Below*) A Japanese 'Navy 0' ('Zero') breaking up in mid-air.

flaps down on the down wind leg getting ready to turn into base
and two Zeros were sitting about two thousand feet above him.
One of them was weaving and the other was starting to drop his
nose and come down and the silly thing was that if he had just
done that, if he'd have dropped his nose and come down, I
guess Scotty would have bought it right then and there. But
what he did was: he pulled up into one of those beautiful stall
turns they liked to do in an attack, he pulled it up and stood it
on its tail and kicked it over at the top and came straight down.
And he gained a lot of speed and I think the problem was that
he didn't realize Scotty had his wheels and flaps down and was
going so damn slow. So he just had time to open fire when he
was starting to overshoot, so he pulled back very hard on the
stick and the next thing I saw was that the two aircraft seemed
to merge together and one of them came out with his wings
folded and the other one was still stooging along with his wheels
and flaps down. What happened was that he'd apparently
hauled back the Zero so violently he'd had a structural failure
because he went on ahead, looked like a goose, folded his wings
and crashed and his Number Two dropped his nose and
actually flamed Scotty.

"The last thing we saw was this Hurricane, smoking badly,
looked like it was on fire, turn and go below the trees. We
thought he'd bought it. We had the air raid and a lot of things
happened about that time but at the end of all of this, took a
good half hour, or an hour, there comes Scotty walking down
the dirt road, and he had his 'chute under his arm and he was
nothing but brassed off with us because we hadn't come to get
him. But of course nobody thought he had the slightest chance
seeing the aircraft go down in flames that low they figured he'd
bought it. But what happened, he said, he'd jettisoned his
canopy, jumped, pulled his chute, it blossomed, the aircraft
crashed, he landed. I really think if records were taken Scotty
probably held the record for the lowest survivable parachute
jump in history!"

My own recollection of this incident tallies reasonably closely
with that of Campbell's

"The only one they caught was (Sergeant) Scott. He was well
into his final approach already over the airfield perimeter and

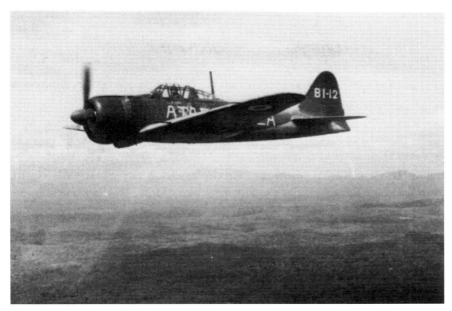

The Nakajima Ki-43 'Hayabusa' fighter.

The Mitsubishi A6 M3 ('Zeke') which was a later
version of the 'Navy 0'.

in fact about level with me as I taxied my aircraft in. I saw, with horror, a Navy Nought on his tail, slim, jungle green, with its disproportionate radial engine and cannon shells thudding from its gun. I saw smoke begin to pour from Scotty's engine and I could even see his head as he hauled back on his stick to give himself height to bale out – and in fact he did succeed and jumping from the aircraft at eight or nine hundred feet landed by parachute safely near the airfield."

This incident was confirmed in the Japanese own records which at the same time make it clear that all of us were wrong in believing the aircraft attacking us were invariably Navy Noughts (Zeros). The two aircraft, the Mitsubishi Zero-Sen and the Nakajima Hayabusa (also known respectively as 'Zekes' and 'Oscars'), were similar-looking machines with only minor differences of wheel farings, cockpit structure and wing shape when seen from above or below, which in the heat of combat one simply did not have the time to notice. Indeed I do not recall that by the time these events were occurring we had ever even heard mention of Hayabusa, or had knowledge that the Japanese possessed fighters other than the Zero.

At all events this incident was recorded in the 'Combat Diary of the 64th Sentai' by Yasuo Izawa, although curiously the Japanese Monographs do not mention this raid. Izawa wrote: 'On the 13th, 29 Hayabusas escorted 7 light bombers to Palembang where Lt. Masabumi Kunii, a veteran and great strafer, pounced on a Hurricane and shot it down, but on pulling out of his dive the wing of his Hayabusa folded like a butterfly and he fell to his death.'

Izawa's account confirms my own clear recollection that Scott had been shot down by the same aircraft which was to lose its wings and not by a Number Two as Campbell recalls. Although with the passage of so many years memories often become dim and confused, there are some which are so etched that they remain sharp and clear. This incident was so to me. I believe I could, even now, pinpoint the exact position of my Hurricane in front of the terminal building at P.1 as, horrified and helpless, I watched one of my friends apparently being slaughtered before my eyes.

There was not, of course, any time just then for comparing

notes. P.1 was a hurly-burly of activity. While the remaining Hurricanes from Java, almost out of petrol, were endeavouring to get out of trouble, those serviceable on the ground were taxiing fast and taking off into the guns of the enemy fighters while above the bombers were making their attack. Ground crews with something to do were, with thudding hearts, helping pilots up into their cockpits and then once their charges were on their way, racing as fast as their legs could carry them to join others who, with no reason to stay exposed to the rain of bullets and cannon shells whistling around the airfield, were already sheltering under the meagre cover of banana trees and light bush on the perimeter. But I recall no panic. There was fear in plenty – there is in fact scarcely anything more frightening than being on the receiving end of a fierce strafing attack directed at one's own airfield. It seems such a personal business! But the ground staffs on P.1 always were magnificent. Unsullied by the shattered morale which gripped Singapore, they were always where they should have been, ready to rearm and refuel their Hurricanes, to start their engines, to get their pilots into the air and even, as the following day was to demonstrate, to turn infantryman and fight the enemy with rifle and pistol.

Surprisingly, the raid of 13 February caused only moderate damage and only light casualties and against the loss of Scott's aircraft and of Pilot Officer Emerton of 232 Squadron (who was last seen being chased over the treetops by enemy fighters) could be set the claimed destruction of two Army 97 bombers and three Japanese fighters and after the enemy had withdrawn northwards, normal squadron operations soon resumed.

These included an afternoon sortie which is worth recounting in that it gives an indication of the frightful flying conditions which were such a hazard to pilots who, with no direction-finding equipment or aids, were flying machines of such limited range as Hurricanes and who at best could maintain only limited radio contact with their base and often had none at all.

It had been reported that enemy flying boats had been seen moored on the west coast of Banka Island and an attack was ordered. Five Hurricanes, led by Maguire, set off, Maguire leading a section of three composed of himself, Thomson and de

Sergeant Pilot A. ("Bertie") Lambert.

la Perelle while Dobbyn (who was later to be shot down and killed in Java), with Lambert as his Number Two, formed a second section to act as top cover. At take-off the weather was poor, over the target area it became very bad and on the return appalling. No flying boats were found and Maguire was to report on his return running into 'one of the best Sumatras I have seen in a long experience and we were lucky to get back without any further loss' while Lambert, more specifically, records:

"As we approached Banka with the leading section probably two thousand feet or so below us the weather worsened and as the leading section lost height to look for the reported target, Dobbyn and I saw them for a time in very poor visibility and then lost contact with them. After searching for some time, the two sections returned to base separately having seen nothing of the flying boats. On our return to base Dobbyn and I had to pass through the centre of a vicious electrical storm. We were thrown about like corks on a rough sea to such an extent that for me to try to keep in formation was simply too dangerous. Two things stick in my mind following this operation: first was a fork of lightning which appeared to go down vertically in front of me right in line with the centre of the airscrew and on appearing over base the intense pall of smoke hanging over P.1 now under very heavy clouds."

So ended operations at P.1 on Friday the thirteenth of February, 1942. The pilots returned to their converted brothel and the ground staff not required to overnight on guard duty, to their half built school or warehouse. No one I have met had any particular recollection of that evening. We pilots would have met in the restaurant above the Luxor Cinema; we would have discussed *ad nauseam* the events of an exciting day; we would have drunk and smoked too much. The ground staff, less favoured, would have done much the same. It was probably thought no more than yet another exciting and memorable day; events were to prove it more significant.

5

Interlude at Sea

Before turning to the events at P.1 and the oilfields at Pladjoe which were to occur on that most dramatic day of all, 14 February, we might pause to consider again the plight of the evacuees from Singapore and especially those of three groups of men and women who were to know such experiences as those who were to survive them would never forget. For the accounts which follow I am grateful for information given to me from many sources but most especially I have to thank Denis Russell-Roberts who not only provided me with photographs to illustrate two of these stories but freely permitted me to paraphrase from his own accounts. I could not more highly recommend the reader who finds these stories as engrossing as I myself have found them, somehow to obtain a copy of Denis Russell-Roberts' absolutely splendid *Spotlight on Singapore* in which they are covered in far greater detail.

The *Mata Hari* was a small coaster of little more than one thousand tons which before the outbreak of the Far East War plied her trade up and down the west coast of Malaya between Singapore and Penang and had as her skipper, Captain A.C.Carston, RNVR, a New Zealander who, beginning his career with the Army in Gallipoli and the Middle East, had spent most of his peacetime life afloat. Shortly before the outbreak of World War II, the Admiralty having taken over his ship, Carston found himself engaged on various escort and patrol duties around Singapore and in the Malacca Straits and after Pearl Harbour these functions were both intensified and extended even up to the harbour of Tonkah in Thailand where he only failed to capture or destroy three Italian ships lying at

Captain A.C.Carston.

anchor by their being scuttled as soon as the *Mata Hari* hove into view.

By the time the decision had been taken to evacuate civilians and key personnel from Singapore, Carston was a veteran and it fell to him to take aboard his tiny vessel almost five hundred passengers of whom approximately one third were women and children. The plan was to quit Singapore on the night of 12 February, sail through the minefields around the island and in the Durian Strait and, hopefully, be sufficiently south of Singapore by first light to avoid the ministrations of enemy bombers. Thereafter the *Mata Hari* would take the swept channel to the west of Singkep Island, continue through the Berhala Strait to the Toehjoeh Islands directly north of Muntok on Banka Island, sail south to the Banka Strait and thence head down to Batavia with the probability of continuing on from there either to India or Australia. It was to be a voyage in which danger from aircraft and submarines was recognized but could they but clear Singapore during the night it was hoped the former might be avoided; and, as regards the latter, with the *Mata Hari* having been equipped as a submarine chaser with depth-charge equipment, Carston hoped to be able to give a good account of himself.

The plan ran behind schedule almost immediately. Following a brush with a party of deserters whose launch had broken down and who endeavoured to stop the *Mata Hari* by raking her with tracer bullets from a bren-gun, Carston proceeded on his way. But quite soon the burning oil from the storage tanks on Singapore and surrounding islets brought about a fog of such intensity that endeavouring to navigate through a narrow channel between thickly sown minefields was not to be contemplated. The *Mata Hari* spent most of that night at anchor. Shortly before dawn, however, Carston decided he must take the risk and proceed so as to be sure of being able to shelter from Japanese bombers by some islet at the southern end of the Durian Strait. This was not achieved as half a dozen bombers discovered the *Mata Hari* shortly after dawn but fortunately their bombs merely straddled her and she escaped almost unscathed and, reaching False Durian Island, hid under the shelter of overhanging mangrove trees.

Late that afternoon, Carston weighed anchor once again, with the intention of reaching the Toehjoeh Islands by dawn on the morning of the 14th. After the early setbacks all seemed to be going according to plan and spirits rose as the ship made her untroubled way through calm and sparkling tropical seas towards escape and safety. However a reminder that a state of war continued was given to the hundreds of passengers crammed, with their luggage, like cattle on *Mata Hari*'s decks when, at nine o'clock that night, flashes were seen as they proceeded along the Berhala Strait which lies between Singkep and Sumatra. Reassuring his charges that these were merely lightning from tropical storms, Carston continued at full power only to observe two hours later a further series of flashes directly ahead. However, having no information that any Japanese naval craft were in the vicinity, Carston continued on his way leaving Berhala Island behind him to the north-west. It was only at about one o'clock in the morning he learnt of the true situation when, remarkably, he was hailed from the pitch-darkness by six survivors from HMS *Scorpion*, a one-time Yangtze gunboat now impressed into the Malayan Auxiliary Fleet, which had been sunk in action with a Japanese cruiser and two destroyers about six hours earlier. From them he also learnt that the *Giang Bee* (which had carried more than two hundred passengers of which less than fifty survived and which had been one of the four vessels which together with *Mata Hari*, *Vyner Brooke* and *Kung Wo* had set out from the Inner and Outer Roads of Singapore almost together) had been sunk. Carston was now able to work out exactly what the series of flashes indicated and that if he proceeded on his present course he would merely run straight into a Japanese fleet.

He had, as he saw it, three alternatives of which, for the best of motives, he was to adopt the worst. He could turn round and head for the Malacca Strait with the intention of rounding the northern tip of Sumatra and then, turning directly westwards, head for India; this would have been a risky thing to do with all the erstwhile Allied airfields in Malaya occupied by the Japanese. He could have headed for the nearby Inderagiri River and made for Rengat which was, of course unknown to him at the time, a staging post for escapers from Singapore; this would have been the right thing to do and his charges would have been got away – but Carston rejected the idea because he had no charts and understood that in any case the Inderagiri was not navigable to craft of the size of the *Mata Hari*. The third, and selected, choice was to head for the mouth of the Moesi River, find a pilot, and take his ship up to Palembang; with no intimation that Sumatra was under any immediate threat of invasion, this seemed the prudent thing to do.

Accordingly he changed course to due south and reached Sumatra's Sakhanah Bay about twenty miles to the north of the Moesi estuary by dawn. It had occurred to him that he might be able to unload his passengers here but he was soon disabused on learning from the master of a fishing boat that the mangrove swamps bordering the bay stretched for many miles inland and that the only passage through them was on tree trunks laid on end whose paths were known only to local natives. Accordingly he weighed anchor and set off for the Moesi. *En route* he and his nervous crew and passengers were much relieved when a huge formation of Japanese bombers passing over them in a westerly direction left them alone – these were, of course, again quite unknown to Carston, the Hudsons and Ki-57s which were delivering the paratroops to P.1.

Arriving, without charts, at the mouth of the Moesi, Carston vainly sought the services of a pilot and it was only late in the evening that he finally discovered there was one aboard a small passing river ship. Dispatching an emissary by small boat, Carston waited, fuming and impatient; but before his emissary returned, searchlights were seen and gunfire heard in the nearby Banka Strait. From the scope of the activity, Carston realized that one of two things was happening – either a naval engagement was taking place or an invasion of Sumatra was in progress. Nevertheless he waited, not daring to attempt the passage up the swift, dangerous, shoaling Moesi without charts or pilot. The emissary at length returned but without the pilot who refused to assist as *he was just about to go on leave in Java!*

Now there were two alternatives: to risk immediate passage up the Moesi; or to attempt, under cover of darkness, to slip through the ships which were rapidly closing Moesi's mouth. Carston decided on the latter. It was a moonless night and the chances of reaching Palembang, or even of making any reasonable headway towards it, were negligible. He would try the sea. But firstly he must make one more decision. If the ships, whose searchlights were now raking the very mouths of the Moesi delta and drawing ever closer, were from enemy ships and the *Mata Hari* was caught and held by them, should he fight or should he surrender? It took him little time to make up his mind. The *Mata Hari*'s armament was pitiful – one 4-inch gun and antiquated Lewis guns. What could he achieve by resistance but the useless loss of nearly five hundred lives? He ordered action stations to be dismissed, struck the White Ensign then ordered full steam ahead ordering a course south-east through the Banka Strait once they had cleared the Moesi shoals.

For a time, astonishingly, things went well. The *Mata Hari* threaded her way unobserved through what Carston soon realized by the narrow occasional pencil beams of searchlights and the dim shapes of vessels he passed by was a major enemy convoy. It could not last. Soon after midnight one of the raking searchlights picked them up, paused, held them. A gun report was heard. Carston ordered the engines stopped and the signals officer to communicate their function. They waited. Five hundred men, women and children waited wondering, tense, afraid. What would it be? A flashed instruction? A megaphoned order? Or the terrible sound of gunfire, whistling shells, tearing metal; the smell of cordite; the heat of flame; the cries of wounded and dying men, women, children? Amazingly it was none of these. After an agonizing ten-minute wait, bathed in the dazzling searchlight beam, the *Mata Hari* was plunged back into darkness. Still they waited, wondering. Nothing happened. The minutes passed. Disbelieving, Carston at length ordered the engines restarted and put to slow ahead. The *Mata Hari* was under way again, creeping through the enemy fleet. Still nothing broke the darkness; still the only sound was the *Mata Hari*'s quietly pulsing engines, the whisper of water against her bows. Seconds became minutes, minutes quarter hours, quarter hours hours. For more than two *Mata Hari* moved on unchallenged, unobserved, her speed gradually increasing, the optimism of her captain and his charges growing. By 3.00 a.m. *Mata Hari* was nearly half-way through the Banka Strait; within two more hours, she would have cleared it. It was not to be. Fate, cruel jade, was only playing games. Suddenly they were again illuminated. This time there was no waiting. In International Code a flashing lamp instructed them to anchor, show lights, not to lower boats.

Yet the play was not quite finished. The searchlight was switched off. There were no more messages; the Japanese, invading Sumatra, had no wish to disturb the secrecy of the night more than was necessary. The *Mata Hari* rode at anchor lit only by the stars and her own few lights, the perfect target if that was eventually to be her fate. It was a long, long wait.

Dawn broke to show a Japanese cruiser less than a mile away. Immediately Carston, last hopes dispelled, ordered all secret documents, collected through the final hour, to be destroyed. The cruiser, guns trained, circled. At any moment either the guns would open fire or a boat would be launched to accept his surrender and take over his ship. Then, most extraordinarily, one of the many launches which had left Singapore appeared. It was a horrifying, yet thrilling stage-play for the passengers crowding the *Mata Hari*'s rails. The launch, HM Launch *311*, commanded by Lieutenant Christmas of the Royal New Zealand Volunteer Reserve and carrying a crew of fifteen and fifty-seven service passengers which, possibly, weaving, twisting, turning, might have escaped, instead gave battle. It was a gallant show but hopeless. Armed with one three-pounder gun there was little of consequence 311 could in any case achieve. But at least she went down with her White Ensign flying; at least she showed the Japanese there was more fight in the enemy than the surrender of Singapore that very day might indicate.

The diversion caused by this tiny episode gave Carston time to dump equipment which might have been valuable to the Japanese overseas and by the time a Lieutenant from the cruiser came over in a boat, a mass of material lay at the bottom of the Banka Strait.

To the nervous passengers the manner of the *Mata Hari*'s being taken over augured well. The Lieutenant behaved with courtesy and correctness, Japanese seamen took charge of bridge, engine and radio room, the anchor was raised and the ship proceeded back to Muntok. Once there the Japanese quitted the *Mata Hari* in the roadstead now crowded with Japanese naval craft and transports. The Lieutenant ordered the Japanese flag run down and the White Ensign hoisted on her for the last time. The next day all aboard her were transferred ashore. Carston was the last to leave. As he did so the White Ensign was slowly lowered and the Rising Sun hoisted in its place. It had all been done with decency and propriety. But it would not be long before things would change. It was not the Japanese Navy which ran the prison and internment camps.

The story of the *Mata Hari* ends sadly but that of the *Vyner Brooke* in tragedy. Commanded by Lieutenant R.E.Burton, RNR, she quitted Singapore about the same time as *Mata Hari*, carrying amongst the evacuees who crowded her decks sixty-four Australian nurses under the command of Major (Matron) Irene M. Drummond of the 2/13th Australian General Hospital. After completing her passage through the Durian Strait she took a different course from *Mata Hari* veering eastwards with the intention of anchoring as soon as she reached Linga Island which lies to the north of Singkep – but, because she had been attacked by Japanese bombers, Burton decided to change this plan and head straight for the Toehjoeh Islands which were reached successfully early the following morning.

Burton now had two choices – to steer eastwards clearing Banka to the north and then, having passed through the Gaspar Strait between Belitung and Banka Islands, head due south for Batavia; or to steer south at once clearing Muntok, sail through the Banka Strait and then head for Batavia on a south-south-easterly course. If anything the former course may have been the slightly shorter one – it would certainly have been safer. Unfortunately, whilst anchored off the Toehjoeh Islands, the *Vyner Brooke* was again bombed and although the attack was unsuccessful, Burton concluded that the most prudent thing to do was to make for Banka Strait the head of which was a mere fifty miles away. For the third time *Vyner Brooke* received attention from Japanese aircraft and this time she was hit with many casualties including two of the nurses, who were killed. The ship sank very quickly and more than a hundred further passengers were drowned. Nine of the nurses were last seen drifting on a raft while twenty-two others, including Sister Vivian Bullwinkel, were crammed with other women in one of the two lifeboats which were serviceable, whilst a number of civilian men and officers and crew of the *Vyner Brooke* swam alongside. In due course this lifeboat reached Banka Island and the weary men and women landed on a beach a mile or two distant from Muntok where they met up with survivors from another ship. An officer set off to negotiate with the Japanese whilst some of the women and children, escorted by a man, set off to walk to Muntok and the Australian nurses stayed behind to care for the wounded. The next morning a Japanese patrol, led by an officer, came upon them, promptly led off the men, marched them round a headland, lined them up at the water's edge and machine-gunned them killing all but a stoker named Lloyd who, badly wounded, feigned death. The Japanese then returned, set up a machine-gun and mowed the women down. Again there was one survivor, Sister Bullwinkel, who, wounded in her dia-phragm, lost consciousness. Recovering consciousness she also feigned death and as soon as she was able to, dragged herself into the cover of the jungle where some days later she was discovered by Stoker Lloyd and some survivors from another ship. In spite of the likelihood that if they gave themselves up to the Japanese they would be massacred, shortage of food and

Sister Vivian Bullwinkel.

Stoker E.A.Lloyd (centre) with two shipmates. Photograph taken in 1941 at Alexandria on completing the evacuation from Crete.

water, and the state of the wounded, obliged them to do so and
they straggled off towards Muntok and, most fortunately
meeting up with a Japanese naval officer, were taken to Naval
Headquarters. Sister Bullwinkel survived the war and (although I have read more than one account to the contrary) so
did Stoker Lloyd.

Lloyd (who had been on HMS *Prince of Wales* when it was
sunk off Malaya) wrote to me of the occurrence forty-two years
later – "One of the officers decided to go to Muntok to
surrender as there were some who were wounded. He came
back later with a platoon of Jap soldiers who with hand signals
split us up into service men and non-service people. They
marched us up to a beach and we were halted in a little bay and
told to turn round to face the sea. All this did not sink in until a
machine-gun was produced and set up behind us. The man on
my right said 'this is where we get it in the back.' I replied 'not
me'. With that the line facing the sea ran forward and dived
into the sea, myself included. The men behind me were shot
and killed and I was hit by four bullets, the last of which hit me
in the head and I must have been knocked out. I awoke hours
later lying on the beach and crawled up into the undergrowth. I
crawled along the beach a few days later and I saw all the
bodies of the nurses in various states of undress and positions. I
thought I was the only one left but found out later that Sister
Bullwinkel and an American journalist were also still alive. I
managed to keep going for a few more days until I was caught
by a Jap patrol."

Another survivor of the *Vyner Brooke* was a Captain Ellen M.
Hannah, now Mrs Allgrove, one of the nurses who, luckily, was
not with the group who were massacred on the beach. She
writes that of the original sixty-five who left Singapore only
twenty-four survived the war.

The story of the third group of men, those aboard the *Li Wo*
must surely rank as one of the finest examples of courage
against impossible odds ever recorded in the war. It was
reported to me by one of its few survivors, then Chief Petty
Officer C.H.Rogers, himself twice mentioned in dispatches.
Rogers was serving on HMS *Repulse* when it was sunk in the
South China Seas and, after a short stint on patrols in the

HMS *Li Wo*.

Jahore Straits, was detailed to join HMS *Li Wo* which was a river boat of about one thousand tons armed with one 4-inch gun mounted forward and two twin Lewis guns. The commanding officer was Lieutenant T.Wilkinson, the First Lieutenant was Lieutenant R.G.G.Stanton DSO, and the total complement numbered about eighty men. After lying at anchor off Keppel Harbour, Singapore, on 13 February, the *Li Wo* set sail at dawn on 14 February. Having been twice bombed, fortunately without being hit, Wilkinson decided to 'make a dash' through the Banka Strait. The balance of the *Li Wo* story can hardly be better told than by repeating verbatim Rogers' own account.

"As we were proceeding to this area, we sighted a convoy of about thirty ships on the horizon off our starboard bow heading in the direction of Banka Island, but could not identify them until we closed into about sixteen thousand yards. Suddenly, well over the horizon and right ahead, the tops of three funnels were sighted which turned out to be those of a Jap cruiser carrying 6-inch guns. We also sighted off our port bow, a Jap destroyer which headed the convoy which was in sections of four and six ships. The captain was now certain that it was an enemy convoy and that its mission was to support invasion. It was then passed round the ship that we were going into action and that the leading ship of the section nearest to us would be the first target.

"Battle Ensign was hoisted (one on gaff and one at mast-head) and we closed rapidly the 4-inch gun being all ready to open fire. With no interference we closed into two thousand yards and then the order 'open fire' was given. The first salvo fell short, the second crossed the bow and the third scored a hit just under the bridge. A cloud of smoke went up and she was set on fire. She turned to port while the remainder turned to starboard and started firing their guns of a small calibre type. The damaged ship was now approaching the *Li Wo* and firing a small type gun. The CO decided to ram her – we hit her at top speed amidships and became interlocked, our bows being buckled back. We were really at close quarters.

"A machine-gun duel took place which was fast and furious, many men being killed and wounded. The *Li Wo* gunners eventually wiped out two guns and this caused the Japs to abandon the ship, which was by this time well on fire. We went full astern. Whilst this was happening, the cruiser had circled around the stern of the convoy and was heading for us at high speed. As we cleared the ship which we had destroyed and set on a course, the enemy cruiser opened fire at our port beam at a range of eighteen thousand yards. We zigzagged as the salvoes fell and we had a poor opinion of the Jap gunners as her salvoes were falling wide – at times three hundred yards or more away. But gradually they came nearer and shrapnel was now hitting us, causing many men to be killed and wounded. I was hit with three pieces of shrapnel in the leg but was not seriously injured. After about the ninth salvo we were told to try and get away and all who were able to jumped overboard. Soon after, the ship was hit on the cordite locker in the rear of the gun and also amidships. The last sight I had of her as she started on her last voyage to the bottom of the sea was something I shall never forget – her ensigns were flying and the captain stood on the bridge, and, although listing to port, she was still under way. Then suddenly she disappeared – the *Li Wo* was no more. For this action Lieutenant Wilkinson was posthumously awarded the V.C."

Chief Petty Officer C.H. Rogers.

With his ship sunk, there was nothing for Rogers to do now but try to save himself. Sighting a lifeboat some distance away, he began to swim towards it but, as he drew nearer, it was rammed by one of the Japanese ships and the thirty or so survivors who had either been in it or hoping to get aboard were massacred by machine-gun fire, hand grenades and "even lumps of coal and wood". However, after a time the ship withdrew and Rogers and seven others, swam to the lifeboat, now half-submerged, and climbed into it. Of these survivors "Lt. Stanton had a bullet hole through the back of his head, another officer was wounded in his stomach and had part of his hand shot away and P.O. Huntley had his foot taken off and was in a very bad condition."

With no oars, many miles from land, and the lifeboat down to the gunwale, a cold, miserable night passed and by dawn the officer Rogers had been nursing died in his arms. Land, about sixteen miles distant, was sighted but there was no way of approaching it. In spite of the presence of sharks, Stanton and a gunnery officer decided to try to swim to a Japanese destroyer sighted about two miles away, Huntley died from his wounds, one soldier was lost overboard and one man set off to try to swim to the shore. There were now only Rogers and two men left in the lifeboat which, now waterlogged, would probably not have supported more. However, towards nightfall a damaged naval whaler was seen and boarded and an intact sail was rigged. As this was being done shouts were heard and seven further survivors from the *Li Wo* on two rafts were seen. Rogers ordered some of these men to be taken aboard and the rest to remain on the rafts which were taken in tow. Eventually, after many hours exhausting rowing which, fortunately, was assisted by a strong wind which had sprung up, almost forty-eight hours after the *Li Wo* had been sunk, the ten weary, hungry survivors reached Banka Island where they were taken prisoner.

6
The Japanese Invade

To survivors of the Sumatran Campaign, Saturday, 14 February, 1942, was to prove the most unforgettable day of their lives. It was to prove a day of incident, surprise, muddle, courage and audacity. Within twenty-four hours boys were to become men and men who had never killed before, who had never, even in wartime, imagined they would kill, would have crossed that line which can never be recrossed. Many would die, some in the air, some in the sea, some in the jungle, some by ambush on the road to Palembang and others, taken prisoner, would be slaughtered by bullet and bayonet in the ditches which ran beside it.

Some twenty minutes before dawn the first of the Hudsons took off from P.2 to attack the invasion fleet. Thereafter the remainder of the Hudsons and then the Blenheims were to take off at intervals of one minute, fly until they reached the Moesi and then along it to its mouth opposite Muntok on Banka Island. Their instructions were to attack the transports (some of which it was expected might already be at the river mouth), rather than the warships. They were to fly at about one thousand feet so as to be low enough for accurate bombing yet near enough to the cloud cover (about as high again) and thus escape the attentions of any Zeros which might be awaiting them.

The convoy was located and attacked but ineffectually. Afterwards some pilots blamed their lack of success on the fact that they only carried two hundred and fifty pound bombs which were too small to sink any of the many vessels which they claimed to have hit. Two Blenheims were lost, shot down by enemy fighters, and six more as well as two Hudsons sufficiently badly damaged as to be put out of action.

No one outside the squadrons knew they were on the way. Ozawa manœuvring his massive fleet and transports off Banka Island did not know; Lieutenant Commander Cooper, onetime senior officer in Guthrie & Co, Singapore, now commanding the minesweeper *Jerantut* moored to the bank of the Moesi River, festooned with camouflage nets and mangrove branches, did not know, nor did his companions Lieutenants Smythe on the *Klias* and Brown on the *Hua Tong*. Eric Sinclair who had escaped from Singapore on the motor vessel *Derrymore* with as a fellow passenger Mr Gorton, a future Prime Minister of Australia, did not know for the *Derrymore* had been torpedoed the previous night and when dawn broke they found themselves, with many others, crammed in a lifeboat which leaked like a sieve in the midst of numerous tiny islets in the Thousand Isles Archipelago off Sumatra. Donald Wright did not know – the *Hung Jow* having passed the night at anchor in the middle of a minefield off Singapore was under way, heading south, with all aboard blissfully ignorant that an invasion fleet lay directly in their path. The New Zealand Flight Commander of 'A' Flight of 258 Squadron, Denny Sharp, did not know – while the co-pilots of his squadron slept uneasily in their brothel, Sharp, having forced landed short of fuel on Singkep Island while on his way from Singapore to P.1 and having crossed by launch to Sumatra, was preparing to set off up the Djambi River. Brigadier Bird in Motor Launch *M.L.433* which had been allocated to him, speeding ahead of Sinclair and proceeding directly towards disaster in the Banka Strait, did not know, nor did the sixty-four Australian nurses on the *Vyner Brooke*. Air Vice-Marshal Pulford and Rear-Admiral Spooner, who had respectively commanded the air and naval forces on Singapore and were heading south to their death on a tiny fever-stricken island in the Rhio Archipelago, and Mr Bowden, the Australian Government Representative in Singapore, whose diplomatic status was not to protect him from the Japanese, did not know. The Dutch Admiral Doorman, still far to the south, gathering his forces, General Bennett, Commander of the 8th Australian Division, ignominiously escaping from Singapore, leaving his troops to their years of captivity and the hundreds of deserters, including the Australians who, armed with Tommy guns and hand grenades, had forced their way aboard the *Osprey* which was to carry both them and Bowden to their deaths, did not know. Brigadier Steele, Chief Engineer of No 1 Australian Corps on his way to examine the contingency plan for the demolition of P.1 but diverted by General Laverack to Oosthaven, the southern port of Sumatra, to see what arrangements were being made for the reception of 3,400 men off the *Orcades* did not know, nor did the men of the 3rd Hussars, already ashore. The ground staffs of the fighter squadrons on P.1 and the RAF ground defence forces under Creegan and Taute who were to be named heroes before the day was through, the Dutch soldiers – 'little more than a Home Guard' – who were not to resist the Japanese and the Achinese Maréchausée (the native troops) who were to give the Japanese a bloody nose, did not know any more than the Dutch civilians, quaking under the mosquito nets of their comfortable beds in their comfortable houses in the better part of Palembang, knew. The workers at Pladjoe whose oil was a glittering prize, vital to her war-machine, almost as important to the Japanese as Sumatra itself and the Dutch Bofors gunners at P.1 and their British contemporaries, the 12th Heavy A.A.Battery with 3.7 anti-aircraft guns at both P.1 and Pladjoe did not know.

No one outside of the airmen and air crews actually involved and those who gave them their instructions knew. For this was the way things were. There was no intercommunication between units. There were only small and totally unco-ordinated groups of Air-Force men, Army men and Navy men, who were each in their own way doing what they could without any sense of fitting into an overall plan of campaign. The only people on 14 February, 1942 who knew exactly what they were about were the Japanese.

Wavell had, on the previous day, reported to Churchill: 'If Southern Sumatra is lost, prolonged defence of Java becomes unlikely . . . From air aspect defence of Java is a hard matter; without Southern Sumatra it is formidable . . . It is clear that retention of Southern Sumatra is essential for successful defence of Java.' The Japanese would hardly have quarrelled

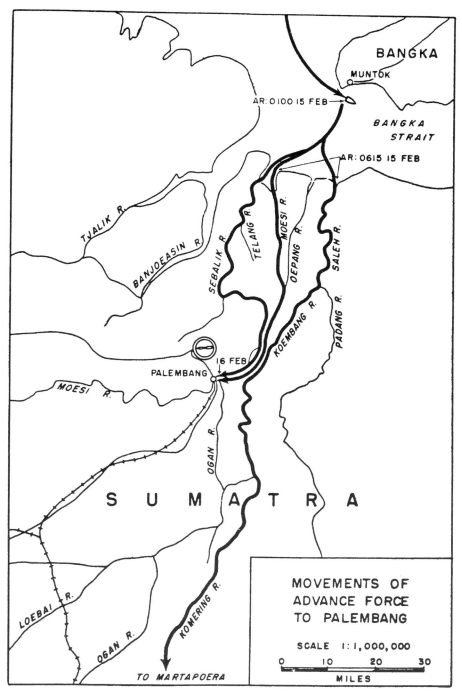

The Moesi River delta and other rivers along which
the Japanese river-borne forces advanced.

with this assessment. Yet, for all their superiority in all theatres of the war, the subjugation of Southern Sumatra presented the Japanese with serious difficulties. It was one thing to transport a superior force of fighting men to the island's shore; quite another to get them to those places which mattered: the oilfields of Pladjoe, the town of Palembang, P.1.

A glance at the map demonstrates their problem. Their three objectives lay some seventy-five kilometres as the crow flies inland from the mouths of the Moesi River which carved its bewildering, wandering way through impassable swamps or land overgrown by jungle stretching for literally hundreds of miles to north and south. There was neither road nor railway. The only conceivable form of attack was by parachutists or troops carried by boat or in self-propelled barges against the current of the fast-flowing Moesi River. And the Moesi would offer no cover – the jungle might be solid to its very bank but did not extend beyond. And it was, like all the main Sumatran rivers, a difficult one with shoals and mud banks which would continually force an attacking convoy from one bank to the other.

Furthermore the Japanese were entitled to believe that if such were their problems, their enemy, being aware of them, would have taken countermeasures – ensuring there were adequate forces at P.1 to defend it against paratroop attacks, providing nasty surprises along the Moesi such as tethered mines, hidden machine-gun posts and sunken blockships and spillages of ignited oil from the very conveniently placed oilfields of Pladjoe and Sungei Gerong on its banks. It seems probable that the very swiftness of their attack, made even before Singapore had fallen, was dictated by their realization that should they delay by even so little as a few days, their reeling foe might recover some equilibrium and set such countermeasures in train.

The Hurricane pilots arrived early at P.1 to be informed that a maximum force was to stand by to escort a formation of bombers which would be attacking an enemy convoy in the Banka Strait. As one of the pilots I have no recollection of being told the convoy was a Japanese invasion fleet. I am certain we had no idea there *was* an invasion fleet; that we had no idea an

Pladjoe and Songei Gerong Oil Refineries on River
Moesi near Palembang.

invasion of Sumatra was imminent. Even granting that forty
years and more have passed since that remarkable day, I
remain convinced that had we known that Sumatra was about
to be invaded, it would have been so etched our memories as
never to have been forgotten. I suppose had we thought the
matter through, we ought to have concluded that a convoy and
an invasion fleet were synonymous, but these were very busy
days, we were very young and mainly concerned with surviving
from one day to the next and invasion fleets arriving un-
heralded were simply not in our philosophy.

At all events we sat strapped in our cockpits waiting for our
bombers to fly overhead. There were fourteen of us, mainly 258
Squadron pilots with, possibly, one or two from 232 Squadron.
This was the maximum number of Hurricanes we ever
succeeded in getting into the air at one time on an actual
operation in Singapore, in Sumatra or in Java. It was also, by
coincidence, the maximum number we were subsequently able
to field for the defence of Java.

The Kawasaki Ki-54. Note the astonishing resemblance to the Lockheed Hudsons below.

Lockheed Hudsons.

Having already given a detailed account of that flight in my book *Hurricane Over the Jungle* (which deals with the entire air campaign through from Singapore to Java) I will merely summarize. The Blenheims did not show and our CO decided we should take off anyway. We flew to Banka and didn't find the convoy – which in retrospect seems inefficient and remarkable. *En route* we were heartened by seeing a large formation of Lockheed Hudsons half concealed from us by a thin skein of cloud, passing a few hundred feet below and heading in the opposite direction. We were wrong to be heartened – they were Japanese aircraft carrying the two hundred and sixty paratroops shortly to be dropped around P.1. and the other hundred to be dropped at Pladjoe. There has been much argument since as to whether these were in fact Hudsons or were Kawasakis which are almost identical in appearance. I have since learnt, by courtesy of Yasuo Izawa (and the Japanese records), that Hudsons (which the Japanese had both bought from the Lockheed Corporation and built under licence) were used.

Lambert (right) and author on readiness.

Izawa states 'On 14 February 1942, 40 Ki-57 ('Topsy') and Lockheed 14 transports with 400 paratroopers, preceded by 27 'Sally' heavy bombers, reached Palembang with a Hayabusa escort from the 64th and 59th.'

As we neared P.1 on the return from our pointless and wasted flight the squadron was instructed not to land at P.1 but to fly on to P.2. Having no R/T (by no means an unusual situation) neither Lambert nor I received this instruction which was given at the same time that I noticed a number of what I took to be Zeros, and were presumably Hayabusas, above. Being unable either by hand signals or frantic wing-waggling to convey this information successfully to Thomson, accompanied by Lambert, I set about engaging the Hayabusas while the balance of the squadron gracefully departed. The next half-hour or more was a busy one during which I was chased twice over Palembang at treetop and rooftop height by Japanese fighters, shot one down, made (I believe unsuccessful) attempts to shoot down two others and finally, almost out of petrol, landed at P.1. to discover it queerly deserted. A few minutes later Lambert joined me. I can assure the reader that it is a uniquely mystifying and disturbing feeling to take off from a

P.1 airfield. The Hurricane in right foreground is positioned approximately where Lambert's would have been after he had landed unaware the airfield was surrounded by paratroops, and the author's Hurricane just to the right of it.

very busy airfield and then to return almost two hours later to find it deserted and silent as the grave. The feeling changes when someone bravely rushes from the cover of the jungle perimeter to tell you why this state of affairs has arisen, that it is surrounded by enemy paratroops. Somewhat hastily, Lambert and I climbed back into our Hurricanes and turned tail for P.2 – which we just managed to reach before running out of fuel.

The majority of personnel who survived believe the para-troop attack to have taken place very early in the day. This is not as I remember; I have always been sure it was quite late on in the morning. Moreover this recollection is supported by my log-book which shows a scramble from P.1 on the 14th which lasted for an hour and took place before the exercise which I have noted as 'Bomber Escort.Banka', by Yasuo Izawa who states 'The paratroopers took to their silks at 1126 hours', and by the Japanese Monographs. And this is, perhaps, an appropriate point at which to study the paratroop drop from the official Japanese point of view.

On the previous day the first group of paratroops had been transported from Sungeipatani, in Malaya, to Kluang and Kahan where they were joined by heavy bombers of the 98th Air Unit and from which 59th and 64th Sentais were already operating, while the heavily escorted convoy carrying the main body of troops was closing in on Banka Island.

February 14th had dawned partially cloudy over Malaya with a cloud ceiling of one thousand metres and visibility varying between ten and twenty kilometres. At 0830 hours the '1st Raiding Unit' of paratroopers took off in forty Ki-57 ('Topsy') and Lockheed 14 transports from Kluang and Kahan airfields and rendezvousing over Batupahat set course in two formations for the mouth of the Moesi River. Ahead of them were twenty-seven 'Sally' heavy bombers escorted by a large number of Hayabusas. There was considerable broken cloud over the P.1 area while at the mouth of the Moesi (which was reached at 1120 hours as planned) the weather conditions, whilst making navigation difficult, helped ensure surprise.

This information is largely drawn from Monograph 69 which is very detailed and there seems little reason to doubt its accuracy up to the point when the paratroops were actually dropped. Thereafter, however, it becomes very romanticized

Japanese War Painting by Miyamoto Saburo entitled 'Divine Soldiers Descend on Palembang'.

and contains many exaggerations and errors. There is a second Monograph No 67 which is a briefer, more considered account, which, with one important exception (dealt with later), accords closely with the facts which can be deduced from Allied sources and it is this Monograph which I have used to cover both the actual paratroop drop and the subsequent ground fighting .

Monograph 67 reads "The day of the airborne assault, 14 February, smoke rising from oil tanks in Singapore spread south and formed smoke screens over Sumatra making it difficult for the crews of the troop-carrying transports to observe the ground. Just prior to reaching the Moesi River area dense fog and clouds were encountered making it necessary to descend to locate the mouth of the river. Having located this check point they continued their course up the river. Visibility over the target area was good. Prior to reaching Palembang, the unit divided – the first echelon for the airfield – the second for the refinery.

"At approximately 1130 hours each echelon jumped. Furious but inaccurate anti-aircraft fire came from both the

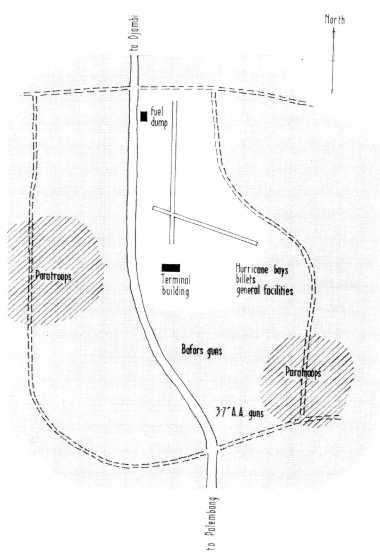

LAYOUT OF P1 AIRFIELD

Sketch plan of P.1 airfield showing location of guns, stores etc and areas where paratroops were dropped. Shaded areas were either swamp, heavy scrub or jungle. Drawn by M.R.Kelly. A.A.Dip. RIBA.

airfield and refinery areas. Anti-aircraft fire shot down one plane carrying equipment for the unit attacking the refinery and forced another carrying troops to land."

I imagine the erroneous belief that the attack took place earlier has arisen because nothing of moment took place until the Japanese arrived and this itself was a sufficiently dramatic happening to have so impressed itself on the minds of those involved as to appear almost to have begun the day.

The immediate protection of the airfield was limited to that which could be given by the Dutch Bofors batteries, the two ack-ack batteries, a few non-flying pilots, perhaps a hundred RAF ground staff – who were in the majority of cases unarmed (the Dutch having, oddly, insisted on disarming them the previous day) – and such of the RAF ground defence as were on duty. This would not mean the entire ground defence of the two fighter squadrons for they were working in shifts on a roster basis so that one group of men and one or two officers would be out on the airfield before being relieved by the other shift coming out from Palembang. Additional to these there were about half a company, perhaps about a hundred, Maréchausée who were not strictly soldiers but a sort of military police. These were native men officered by Dutchmen most of whom were in the town at the time of the paratroop drop and either could not or did not attempt to get out to the airfield once it was known it had been attacked.

The senior officer for P.1 was Group Captain Darley and immediately junior to him Wing Commander Maguire, Officer Commanding the originally proposed wing of 232, 242, 258 and 605 Squadrons, who had been asked by Darley (who happened to be sick that morning) to take charge for the day. With Maguire were the Defence Officers of 232 and 258 Squadrons, Flying Officers 'Paddy' Creegan and 'Bill' Taute. Pilot Officer 'Micky' Nash, one of the 258 Squadron pilots, was Duty Officer for the day and a number of other 258 pilots (who were not required to be at the airfield as there were insufficient Hurricanes left for all pilots to be on readiness) were in the town, as were a few pilots of 232 Squadron. Amongst the 258 pilots in Palembang were Campbell, Macnamara, (Sergeant) Scott, Milnes and Cicurel and also the Engineering Officer,

Tudor Jones.

Maguire (now Air Marshal Sir Harold Maguire) has prepared an account for me of the day's affairs as he remembers them:

"We got the Hurricanes off fairly early in the morning and about twenty minutes later we saw the first Japanese parachute carrying aircraft heading towards Palembang town. A series of them headed over the airfield. They were engaged by the two British anti-aircraft batteries, both Welsh, one heavy and one 20 mill light Ack Ack but as far as I could see with the usual thing of fuses going off at the wrong altitude. I saw no casualties as a result of anti-aircraft fire although some of them did swing about a bit and as a result the parachutists were dropped rather irregularly mostly to the south of the airfield. Some were dropped to the east and there were some overshoots to the west. Later on these gave a certain amount of trouble from their habit of hiding themselves in trees and sniping with a good field of fire. There was, as you can imagine, a certain amount of confusion.

"I went down the road to see if it was still open about an hour after the parachutists had dropped and it was at that time, although people had been fired on travelling up and down. I then went back and found that we had no means of communication at that stage with Palembang 2 for what reason I'm not sure and we did reconnect after a bit and until about twelve o'clock when communications were broken finally again. We tried to recall the aircraft that were airborne to deal with the raiders but I think they didn't have fuel or didn't get back in time. And about this time we learnt that all aircraft airborne were to return to P.2. On learning this I decided that the groups of airmen trying to repair aircraft in exposed positions on the edge of the jungle at P.1 should be withdrawn. Most of them were unarmed and I thought they could be much more usefully employed at P.2.

"I'm not sure at this stage how many troops were actually on Palembang 1. There were the RAF Regiment people – then called Air Defence – and there were the Dutch Maréchausée, but most of their officers were in the town. The couple who were there were Indonesians and spoke only Indonesian, and obviously Dutch, so our communications with them were poor;

Air Marshal Sir Harold Maguire CBE OBE DSO.

but they were asked to guard the Northern side, where they had indeed their own slit trenches and so forth, and this they did until we left finally. I formed up the troops we thought we could spare, told them (those without transport) to try to walk into the town and keep in the rubber on the right-hand side of the road and not go aimlessly down the road itself. We sent some armed parties with them down the road to act as some form of protection. I gather that some of these parties got through and some were ambushed and quite a few were lost as a result or wounded. One of the New Zealand pilots, whose name unfortunately I can't recall, did magnificent work going up and down the road, giving information from the town, picking up wounded and troops who'd missed their way.

"About mid-morning we were getting sniping fire and some machine-gun fire from the south and west of the airfield and Bill Taute went with a small hand-picked party to deal with the sniper fire to the west which he did very successfully and Creegan (who was in command of the air-force men) and I had a conference to decide where we would concentrate those forces which were properly armed and properly led. We decided to concentrate on Air Traffic Control and an arc where there were anti-aircraft trenches around it. And this we did. At this point I decided that all outlying aircraft which were badly damaged and could not be easily repaired should be destroyed. And this was done by a party of volunteers and done effectively. We dragged in all those aircraft we thought there was hope for nearer the protected zone. We got all transport that we could gather – it wasn't very much, I think it was about three lorries – and parked that also in the protected area. All the time we passed as many troops as we could, those that were not needed for protection, and these later batches, I think, from what I could hear later, were more successful because by this time they joined up with the anti-aircraft people who had also destroyed their guns and marched in a formed up body to Palembang."

Bill Taute, in peacetime an architect, was a South African and therefore particularly useful having a command of Dutch. He had been ground defence officer of 258 Squadron in UK under its (and my) previous Commanding Officer, a New Zealander, Squadron Leader Clouston, who, by a strange coincidence, was in Palembang at this time having just got away from Singapore to which he had been posted recently. Taute's recording on the whole very much confirms the accuracy of Maguire's account

Flying Officer 'Bill' Taute MC.

"I think the idea was there would always have to be a properly constituted group of men on the airfield manning such gun positions as we had, there shouldn't be any gaps, whether it was night or day. I suppose it was probably divided into three shifts of eight hours. Something like that. You did what you could to make sure that you had machine guns – we didn't have too many. Or Lewis guns which are pretty useless. We had two Vickers Maxims – you know, the things with the belt. They weren't too bad – they were I suppose 1914, or 1918, vintage. Anyway we had them. And there were one or two Bofors manned by the Dutch in properly built emplacements. The Army, that's the British Army, were represented by two 3.7 Ack Ack positions. One on the southern edge of the airfield – quite a distance away, not sitting on the end of the runway. Maybe half a mile away. And the other one on the northern side. And that was the sort of defence we had. And we had to liaise with the Army. Don't ask me their names, I couldn't tell you. They were British Ack Ack gunners and they'd built their own emplacement. I went to see it. That side of things was my particular stamping ground. They'd converted it into a properly entrenched, sandbagged gunpit.

"We didn't have a very good air raid warning system. It was a thing that happened by somebody sitting in the rubber miles away with a telephone line and we were warned by the rather antediluvian arrangement that if and when aircraft came into attack a red flag would be run up on the Headquarters building. On the Control Tower. The day they dropped the paratroops I had just arrived on the airfield with my group to take over from the night shift and I suppose it must have been about eight o'clock, maybe eight-thirty, and we were in our various positions and then this red flag ran up on the Control Tower and probably a few minutes later we saw aircraft approaching from the north and we immediately identified them as being Hudsons. They looked like Coastal Command Hudsons. So we didn't think very much about it. We thought they're friendly aircraft, our own aircraft. And then they circled slowly round. And then we realized there were fighter aircraft with them which looked like Japanese Navy Zeros. And then the parachutes began to drop and they were different colours. There were white ones and one or two I think orange ones.

They fell beyond the perimeter of the airfield and where we were, we were between them and the airfield.

"So I then decided that the best thing to do was to go and find them. You couldn't find them all but you could go and find them where you thought there were some of them. And they were in the area of this Ack Ack gun, this 3.7 to the south. There was a lot of noise going on because the gunners in their Bofors pits were shooting off their little popguns and some of our Maxim boys had a go with their Vickers Maxim but they didn't hit anything. So I gathered as many men as I could get and we set off through this perishing pineapple plantation. Ever walked through a pineapple plantation in a hurry? My God, it's a painful procedure! Those damn leaves are as sharp as needles. They cut you. You didn't have time to walk between the rows. You were heading for a certain point, obliquely across to that point, so you had to more or less jump over the plants. We got into some bits of jungle and Ha! Ha! some of the men began to jump up and down, screaming and beating their legs and their feet and their crotches! There were red ants amongst them! It's amazing how painful that can be – when a red ant gets you by the balls! You know what's hit you! They were big ants, they really bit!

"Anyway we finally got where we could hear some shooting going on. There were some Japanese paratroopers up in trees firing at this gun emplacement and so we more or less made, I suppose you'd call it a semicircle around this thing, and shot a few of these fellows. Came tumbling out of the trees. That was very satisfactory. Because although you knew damn well there were plenty more where those came from, at least you were knocking some of them off. And then we couldn't find any more. There didn't seem to be any more and yet there was shooting going on. So we decided they were on the other side of this gun emplacement and we came out on a path which was a sort of beaten track which led from the gun emplacement, round to the western side of the airfield and then back to the Headquarters building. And shooting up and down that path there was a lot of stuff being flung around.

"Anyway I decided what we really needed to knock these fellows out was a machine gun of sorts so I sent two men, a Corporal and a Sergeant, to fetch the Vickers. While they were away we kept trying to find where the Japanese were firing from. We couldn't see, it was pretty dense jungle – I think what they did was to climb up sufficiently high in the trees to see the gun emplacement and then to shoot at it. As you know firing a modern rifle there's no smoke like you could see in the old days, there's no flash so you really can't see things coming. All you could hope to do was ooze around in the jungle until you could see a Japanese, which we did occasionally, and then you could shoot him and then he'd fall out of the trees. And then the two men came back with the machine gun. We put it up on the edge of the road and just then a whole group of Japanese came storming up the road, they couldn't have known we'd brought up a machine gun at that moment and so we gave them a bit of a fright. They soon disappeared. Then all the shooting stopped and we imagined, all right they've gone away, they've had enough for the moment. Whereupon we were able to go along to the gun emplacement, out came the Captain in charge, thanked us very much, if it hadn't been for us etcetera and while we were standing there congratulating each other, thinking this is all very good, by this time of course hours had gone by. It's curious you don't realize how much time has gone by.

"Then haring up the road came a jeep and in it was our own CO Maguire. And he began to give me a proper dressing-down for not being nearer the airfield. All this, what was I doing sitting up here drinking tea or beer or whatever it was? So the Captain in charge then put him straight and said – 'You've got it all wrong. These people came along and saved us from being slaughtered by the Japanese.' So Mac said: 'Oh, good. Well then that's fine. Well you'd better come back now, you've done your job. What are you going to do with that gun?' 'Oh,' he said, 'we'll make it useless. We'll spike it.' Or do whatever it is you do to guns that weren't any use any more. 'And then we're going to pack it in and go into Palembang.' So then Mac told me: 'Oh, by the way, you'd better come back to the Head-quarters building. We'll decide what to do. And, on the way, just set fire to the petrol dump.' "

One of the officers with the ack-ack guns on P.1 was a Lieutenant Simpson who explained to me that his Battery was originally intended for the Middle East but on the outbreak of

Servicing a Hurricane at P.1. This would have been
done away from the runways and probably in the
area close to the ack-ack gun posts.

the Far East War the convoy was split into two parts when at
Durban, one continuing on to its original destination of Basra
and the other to Singapore via the Sunda Straits (which lie
between Java and Sumatra) arriving about two weeks before
the island fell. Their ship was the SS *Monarch of Bermuda*. After
a few days they were seconded to Sumatra being transported on
overcrowded Straits Settlement ships which, running the
gauntlet of heavy bombing unscathed, travelled up to the town
of Palembang by the Moesi River. Once established, in sparse
accommodation at the airfield, they found the task of trying to
engage enemy aircraft with 3.7 guns over open sights (much of
the equipment which would have been needed to connect the
guns with the command post having been shipped on to Basra)
an impossible one although they did manage to record shearing
off the wing of a Zero and finding the half charred body of its
pilot in the jungle. Lieutenant Simpson's account was interesting in that he states that the Hudsons which carried paratroops
had RAF roundel markings on them.

Another witness was Bombardier East who at the time the aircraft transporting the paratroops arrived (which he gives as between 10 and 11 a.m.) was supervising the loading of stores from the coastal steamer *Ipoh* about half a mile from the refinery at Pladjoe where the Left Troop of his Battery was stationed. An air raid warning had been given but as the aircraft were recognized as Hudsons, fire was not opened up on them, and it was only when the refinery was suddenly strafed by low-flying Zeros and almost at once they saw paratroops descending on the refinery they realized what was happening. At once his Commanding Officer, Major Coulson, called Headquarters men together, issued them with rifles and ammunition and rushed them to the dropping zone. They claimed to have successfully mopped up this group of about one hundred paratroopers in a five-hour engagement in the course of which amongst their casualties was a Captain Sherrington who was killed. But now they were informed that Japanese troops were coming up the Moesi in invasion barges (this must either have been on the morning of 15 February or rumour had pre-empted

The residential quarters at Pladjoe with oil storage tanks to rear – the scene of very bitter fighting.

fact) so it was decided that the Oil Tank Farm and Refinery should be blown up, an operation which took quite some little time to carry out as the men had to be instructed on how to use gun-cotton and where to place the charges for the best results. When all was prepared all the men save half a dozen, who included East, withdrew to Palembang. The charges were then set off and, so East was informed, by the time the invasion barges began to reach the refinery the ensuing blasts of the petrol and diesel oil tanks flooded out on to the river and the burning fuel carried downstream on the six-knot current engulfed the best part of a section of the invasion force.

A.H.C.Roberts of the same battery confirms this noble effort: "We had reasonable success wiping out the first attack. But the Japs saturated the area with more paratroops and an invasion force up the river. On orders from the Dutch we slowly fell back to the river bank allowing the Japs to occupy the refinery. We suffered many casualties in the process. The Japs commanded the area all around them by setting up machine-gun posts on top of the storage tanks filled with high octane aircraft fuel. What we didn't know, and neither did the Japs, was that incendiary bombs had been planted in all the storage tanks. These were all ignited at the same time and we beat a hasty retreat to the other side of the river but even there the heat was intense. Fighting a rearguard action back towards the coast we never saw the tropical sun for four days, so intense was the fire and smoke from the burning refineries."

Roberts' account is confirmed by Captain P.H.S.Reid who was awarded a military OBE for outstanding services whilst a prisoner of war in the Far East: "The oil refineries were mainly burnt out and suffered from explosions during the fighting with paratroops especially when at Pladjoe (Shell) refinery, a Dutch Kapitein Ohl launched a 68 grenade attack and set the place in flames; Sungei Gerong N.K.L.M. was destroyed by means of a time fuse bomb. The Japs had the refineries partly working, of course, soon after, but even today (March 1975) Pladjoe is still partly out of action."

The Japanese account of these events is given in Monograph 67:

"The first echelon, as planned, dropped troops on both sides of the airfield. Following reorganisation they engaged the enemy in numerous small skirmishes. The enemy had been taken by surprise and his resistance was marked by confusion. Shortly after the landing the element which had dropped south-west of the airfield attacked enemy reinforcements moving along the highway from Palembang. The lead automobile in this convoy was overturned and the remaining enemy troops retreated towards the city. [This statement is the only erroneous one in the Monograph – the vehicle overturned had been leaving P.1 for Palembang.] The terrain surrounding the airfield was covered with dense jungle except for open spaces along the road. Both sides encountered great difficulty in employing troops in mass under such conditions; and, as a result, hand-to-hand combat was the rule throughout the operation . . .

A recent photograph of the Djambi to Palembang road, taken close to the airfield, on which many of the Allied casualties occurred. At the time this was a much narrower dirt road, badly drained and pot-holed.

"In the meantime, the second echelon which also was divided into two elements dropped in the vicinity of the refinery. The elements which dropped west of the tributary of the Moesi had the misfortune to land in the swampy area south of the refinery. They overcame this initial handicap and succeeded in infiltrating the refinery, but only after stiff resistance from the enemy. It was not until the following day that the enemy withdrew and the entire refinery [was] occupied. The destruction of the machinery was slight, permitting immediate utilization of the refinery.

"The platoon which dropped east of the tributary was partially frustrated in its attempt to capture intact refinery installations as enemy incendiaries fired from the north bank of the Moesi set the installation afire. Later investigation proved the damage only superficial and the main equipment repairable."

Tom Jackson. (Front row third from left). Photograph taken shortly after arrival following terrible voyage from Java to Japan on SS *Dai Nichi Maru*. This camp, where author also spent most of his captivity, was known latterly as 'Hiroshima 5'.

None of the events occurring at Pladjoe and Sungei Gerong were, of course, known to the beleaguered defenders at, and would-be escapers from, P.1 and even had they known it is doubtful if they would have been particularly interested – they had matters much closer at hand to occupy their minds. There was not one man amongst them who survived who did not have a story on which to dine out for the rest of his life. An example of these is told by Aircraftman Tom Jackson, one of the 605 Squadron ground staff who kept a diary and wrote of 14 February:

"I went to the 'drome to dig trenches this morning. The alarm went at about five to nine. The signal for an air raid was a red flag hoisted on the watch tower flag pole. If you didn't happen to be looking you didn't know one way or the other. We kept on working and were just saying 'It's time for breakfast' – we had started before breakfast time – when we heard aeroplanes approaching. We couldn't see anything for a while and we just sat on the top of our trench and waited, ready to dive at the first sign of trouble. Eventually we heard engines and then we saw the machines. Twelve twin-engined bombers heading straight for the 'drome and if they kept on they would pass right over our heads. Everybody piled into the trench. I got my camera out and waited on top. I wasn't much worried because I knew I would be able to see any bombs falling and have time to dive then. I took one picture as they approached the edge of the 'drome and one as they were overhead. It was then I saw that they were Blenheims!

"Half an hour later we heard more engines and we just went on working thinking it was the Blenheims again. Somebody looked up and remarked: 'Oh it isn't the Blenheims, it's a shower of Hudsons.' We all looked down the 'drome to where the aircraft were breaking cloud and going across the bottom end of the strip. As we looked we saw several white dots appear from the machines. The dots grew and became parachutes. 'Hell's teeth! Paratroops!' I took three photographs of this amazing sight and then I had to duck. Jap bombers came and pasted the 'drome and then fighters appeared and strafed the dispersal points. Seven of the chaps decided to run for it up to the watch office.

"What a commotion! Bombs, bullets, shrapnel and the

knowledge that there were hundreds of Japs not above a few hundred yards away made us a bit shaky. We wondered why our rifles had been taken from us! I was with 'Pug' Watson, another wireless bloke. We decided that the thing to do was beat a hasty retreat. As the only other alternative was to square up to the invaders with a camera and two steel helmets, we didn't take long to decide the point. We nipped into the jungle at the side of the strip with the intention of getting up to the watch office where we hoped we'd be reasonably safe. I wish to hell I had never gone into the jungle! Our first difficulty was in getting over the barbed wire which was lying just inside the tangled mass of trees and shrubs. It didn't hold us up for long though and soon we were in the midst of really thick stuff. We could hear the war going on outside, the roar of machines strafing the 'drome, the heavy A.A. guns, small bursts of machine gun fire and occasionally the drone of a bomber followed by the crump of exploding bombs.

"It wasn't long before we were in a sorry mess. Clothes torn, bodies scratched, and cheesed off to the teeth. Ankle deep in sludge and slime all the time and occasionally up to the knees, wading through water and semi-swimming the deep bits, scratched by the sharp bits, whipped by the springy bits and held back by the tough bits! We struggled for four hours to get about half a mile. We must have gone miles out of our way. When we reached the edge of the 'drome again we ran across the strip and lay for a minute to get our breath back. "Pug" met one of his pals a few minutes later and I headed for the spot in the woods where breakfast had been left. When I reached the place I took one look and left immediately. The place was smothered in blood. A bomb had burst on the group of chaps cooking the grub and milling around it in general and killed several of them. Nobody seemed to know anything, as per usual, and I got on a push bike and went down the road to Palembang. I hadn't gone very far when I was stopped by an Army Officer who wanted to know: 'Where the hell I was going to!' I replied that I hadn't the faintest notion at which he blew up in the air. He told me the Japs had an ambush a little further down the road at a corner where they had blown over a heavy lorry which was taking wounded into Palembang and that I would have sailed gaily on to it and been potted. I joined a small group of RAF blokes in an army camp at the side of the road and waited. We were supposed to be in a slit trench because of the bullets which kept whistling through the trees, but nobody seemed to think that the bullets were anything to do with them and we sat on the edge of it.

"It was a rather strange affair altogether. I personally didn't seem to be connected with the war that was going on around me at all. After a wait of some thirty minutes or so, volunteers were called for to carry shells to the 3.7 A.A. guns which represented the aerodrome defence. Two or three of us went and were given one large lump of shell each. To get to the gunpits we had to go down a sleeper path which was being sniped at. So we had to wriggle along pushing the shell in front. It seemed like a mile from the road to the gun position. When we reached it the gunners showed us rifle bullets embedded in the big tyres of the guns. The guns were firing at point-blank range at the Radio Location van about seventy-five yards away. They couldn't reduce the fuses sufficiently to blow it up and were just pumping shell after shell into it to try and set it on fire. The Japs were between the van and the gun pits.

"We went back for a second load and after it had been delivered were told the guns were to be evacuated. We went back to the camp and hung around for a little while until someone realized that because of the ambush the guns wouldn't be able to get through to Palembang. It was decided to try and get past the corner. It was known native troops had gone into the jungle to get behind the strong post but the exact situation wasn't known. A large Army car, a sixteen horse-power affair, was filled with petrol and checked over and a mixed collection of Army Officers, N.C.O.s and men piled in armed to the teeth with rifles, revolvers and one Tommy gun. I was in the back still with my camera and tin hat but no arms. With rifles poking out of all the windows and the luggage boot, we set off."

7
Outside the Ring

Away from the field itself there was, meanwhile, much activity in the air, on water and in the town. The Hudsons and Blenheims based on P.2 flew continual but largely unsuccessful sorties against the invasion force. Many pilots and machines were lost, either shot down by the attendant Japanese fighters or destroyed by the fierce anti-aircraft fire from the naval ships and transports. Even amongst those which managed to return to base, many were so badly damaged as to be unable to take any further part in the proceedings. It was indeed a grim business counting the number of machines returning, dragging the dead and dying from amongst those which had, watching others which had limped back somehow, crash on landing. To the crews who survived it was doubly frustrating having to compare the Japanese success in sinking within forty minutes the *Prince of Wales* and *Repulse* with their own failure to achieve through a long, bloody and expensive day anything of significance. Plenty reiterates the main reason for this lack of success was that the only bombs provided for them in this theatre were the two hundred and fifty pounders. As he was to express it: 'We might as well have dropped marbles for all the damage the two hundred and fifty pounders achieved.' It is certainly probable that had P.2 possessed a squadron or so of torpedo carrying-aeroplanes which could have attacked at first light or used the cover of the early morning mist or afternoon bad weather, the Japanese would have had greater problems.

The Hurricane pilots were busy too and the account given by Doug Nichols, one of the 258 Squadron pilots, is typical of their experiences:

Sergeant Pilot Doug Nichols in cockpit of his Hurricane after he had escaped to Colombo. Photograph taken after Nichols had received his commission.

"I remember climbing at almost stalling speed right underneath a formation of Jap bombers with a top cover of Zeros. And all I could do was hang on the stall and give one of the bombers a very good burst before finally stalling out and going off in search of my Number Two who had disappeared. I decided to get away from the aerodrome. I'd been flying at about four hundred feet and wanted to get some height. I went to the west of the airfield where I saw a bit of a dogfight going on and there was one lonely Hurricane – who it was I don't know; I think it was my Number Two – he was going round some of this small cumulus stuff, sailing innocently around with about three Zeros ready to jump him and I went into the attack but unfortunately I hadn't seen about three more Zeros about a thousand feet higher than I was and they came from round the back of these clouds and clobbered me and I baled out. And I landed in a swamp. I clattered through some trees and landed in some very marshy ground which turned out to be the edge of a little island and I wandered off in three or four different directions but came to deep water every time. And I'd done something to my ankle so that I could hardly walk and I tried to find a place to sleep. I found an old rubber drying hut but the mosquitoes became so bad that I set off again and eventually found a kind of log walk across part of the swamp and I came to some more dry land, still in thick jungle, very thick undergrowth, with old neglected rubber trees.

"Occasionally I fired my pistol and, after a long time, there was an answering shot from a distance. With paratroops all around the place I then wondered if I'd been rather unwise and I thought even more so when eventually, out of the trees, came these little brown fellows with their funny hats and their tightly putteed uniformed legs, all of them pointing rifles at me. And I thought, I have made a boo boo here! But fortunately they were Dutch troops and they had a white officer in charge and he took my revolver and dressed the wound on my leg and they carted me, half hopping, half walking, to a truck about seven miles away and eventually we got back nearly to Palembang only to find that we couldn't get back to the aerodrome because it was cut off. Somehow or other, I joined up with Ambrose Milnes and we were told, by Vic Perelle I think it was, that we couldn't get to the airfield and we would have to look after ourselves and make our own way back to Java."

Meanwhile Cooper and Smythe under their mangrove-festooned camouflage nets at the mouth of the Moesi were also far from idle. Cooper writes:

"About 11.00 a.m. some fifty odd aircraft appeared overhead. It soon became obvious that it was an attack on Palembang and one or two aircraft peeled off. Unfortunately I was in the process of transferring what few charts we had to Brown, the captain of the *Hua Tong* as I had spent three nights on the bridge and my sub-lieutenants were very raw. The *Hua Tong* (an ex-river steamer from the Yangtze) was in the process of towing my boat up to my own ship when we were bombed. The *Hua Tong* was hit on the fo'c'sle and my boat was overturned. I paddled my upturned boat to shore with my coxswain and two ratings and we reached the mangrove swamps which to my horror contained more snakes than I have ever seen in my life before or since. Two or three passes were made at us by aircraft with machine gun attacks and as soon as it was over we managed to refloat our boat and returned to the *Jerantut*. We broke radio silence and were ordered to return to Palembang."

This account is confirmed by Lieutenant Smythe, who in civilian life had been a member of the staff of Mansfield & Co of Singapore, Blue Funnel Line – Agents and Managers of the Straits Steamship Co. – and who, in the March preceding the outbreak of the Far East War, had been appointed Commanding Officer of HMS *Klias* a coaster of some 209 tons which had been converted into a minesweeper. The *Klias* (one of the ships which went to the assistance of the *Empress of Asia* which, crowded with troops, had been bombed and sunk off the western entrance to Singapore and which had been intensively engaged in minesweeping through the Durian and Rhio Straits off Singapore) was one of the two small vessels which had accompanied the *Jerantut* to Banka, the other one being, of course, the *Hua Tong*.

Meanwhile the large armada of small craft evacuating the VIPs and deserters from Singapore were rapidly approaching the danger area still blissfully unaware of what lay in store for them. Amongst them was of course the *Hung Jow* carrying Donald Wright and his twelve companions. But they were fortunate indeed! Events occurred which were to cause their skipper to change his plans of sailing to Java and thus avoid

Lieutenant Colonel
Donald Wright.

running into the trap of Banka Strait

"Now at about nine o'clock the bombers started to come over in flights of ten and twelve but we were such an insignificant little target that they didn't worry us – or that was our assumption. This was so for a time but later in the day another flight of twelve came over, and they went straight over the top of us and we thought we were safe and then four, the last four, broke off, turned round and came for us. We thought our number was up but they flew straight over us and went for a small merchant boat on our port side which they hit. We immediately turned round to see if we could give assistance and found that she was in a very sad way and there were many wounded on board. We therefore pulled alongside and agreed we would take as many wounded as possible on our little boat and our fit people would get on to the damaged merchant vessel. However at that moment there was a cry and four bombers were then seen approaching the vessel. We cast off and were less than a hundred yards away when these bombers released their bombs and hit the merchant vessel in the exact spot where we had been only minutes before. The boat now sank.

"The bombers turned and then came for us. We went as fast as we could, a full, I should think, fifteen knots, zigzagging as much as possible and they dropped bombs and missed us. They then turned and made towards Singapore and we assumed that all their bombs had been used up. We picked up all the wounded we could from the water and another boat then appeared, very much bigger than us, and took all the fit people on board. We said we would go to the nearest place possible and drop the wounded and get such attention as we could find for them. This left our little boat so overloaded that no one dare move from port to starboard, or vice versa for fear of upsetting the whole caboose. Luckily the weather was fine and the water really quite glassy and about nine o'clock that evening I suddenly heard a voice in the dark saying: 'Can you give me a lift?' which was repeated. We shone a torch on the water and saw there a bod lying on a Lilo. [This 'Lilo' would in fact have been the dinghy fighter pilots carried under their parachutes.] He paddled himself alongside and got on board. He was a pilot named Puckridge who had been shot down and he said, quite nonchalantly: 'By Jove, it was lucky I heard you. I've just been having a good sleep.'

"Now the intention of our skipper, who was an RNVR Sub-Lieutenant, had been to try and make Batavia but, as there were now so many on board, he decided he wouldn't make it and we tried for the Inderagiri River which was not very far away. We hoped that if we went up this river we might find a hospital for all the wounded that we had taken on board . . ."

That was more than a good decision – it was the only decision the Sub-Lieutenant could have taken which offered the chance of freedom.

Meanwhile, the New Zealander, Flight Lieutenant Sharp

The five remaining New Zealanders of 258 Squadron. Left to right: P/O Bruce McAlister (killed in Singapore), Flt Lt Victor de la Perelle, Flt Lt D.J.T.('Denny') Sharp, F/O Harry Dobbyn (killed in Java), P/O Campbell White. Originally 258 Squadron had been largely composed of New Zealand pilots.

(who, it will be recalled, having force-landed his Hurricane on Singkep Island and then made his way across to Sumatra with the intention of rejoining 258 Squadron in Palembang), had reached the mouth of the Djambi River:

"Next morning we weighed anchor and we edged along the coast. The skipper knew where he was going, but it took him quite a while to find it. But eventually he found the stakes which marked it, this river, and he turned in and to me he was just steering towards a mangrove swamp. But nevertheless eventually we entered this river and we'd gone about half a mile from the mouth and there was what was obviously a fishing village because they had all sorts of dugouts and things like this and we pulled in beside there on a little jetty and what we were after was cigarettes. We went ashore and sure we were able to get some cigarettes. But it was a muddy, filthy village and I felt sorry for the inhabitants. It was very low lying and the level of the land on which all these houses were constructed was only about two, maybe three metres at the most, higher than the level of the water.

"Okay, we set off from there and this was fairly early in the morning – about eight, nine o'clock, and it was not a very interesting river because jungle or mangroves came right down to the sides and it was winding and muddy and you could never tell how deep it was. It varied in width from I'd say about one hundred and fifty yards down to about seventy-five yards and occasionally we passed one of these villages that we'd met at the mouth. So anyway we arrived in Djambi late in the afternoon, about five, six p.m. The first thing I did was to congratulate the crew and thank them very much for what they did for us and gave them some cigarettes – I didn't have any money – and said I'd make their name known to the Governor. And the next thing was to go to the Governor. So I contacted the Governor in this little town of Djambi and the reason I contacted him of course was that I wanted some assistance to get some transport and drive straight down to Palembang and rejoin the squadron.

"Well it was okay. I got some money from the Governor. I had to sign a chitty for it and we went that night and stayed in a sort of guest house like they have in India . . ."

While Sharp was exercising all his energy trying to get to

Palembang, in the town the Dutch were exercising theirs in trying to get out of it, while their panic was balanced by uninterest amongst the native population. It no more seemed to occur to the majority of the Dutch that any obligation rested with them to resist the Japanese than it had occurred, or in due course would occur, to the civilians in Java. Unlike their colonial contemporaries, the British, the Dutch did not regard their East Indian possessions as mere staging posts in a career but as places in which to live and die. The young bachelor executive would return to his native Holland to find himself a wife and then return with her to Java, Sumatra, Bali or some other island there to raise a family and, most probably, there to be one day buried. In consequence the towns, or at least those parts of them where the Dutch lived, were built as garden cities in which could be found comfortable, spacious, trimly presented homes, wide straight streets, splendid flower-bedecked hotels and magnificent restaurants where the burghers – astounding trenchermen – and their wives polished off enormous *Rijstaffels* and quaffed huge quantities of beer.

It did not seem to occur to them to contemplate what would happen to these jewels of possessions or what their position would be if the Japanese won the war. Having given up hope that the British, Australians and Americans would work some last-minute miracle and pull their chestnuts from the fire, their philosophy seemed to be to bury their heads in the sands of their current comfort and assume it would all turn out well in the end and the only sensible course meantime was to do nothing which might bring down the wrath of the Japanese on their heads. All this will no doubt be hotly denied by the Dutch but the evidence is unassailable. This is not, of course, to say that there were not exceptions. Naturally there were. The Dutch Navy, for all its failure to do anything useful so far as the attack on Sumatra was concerned, was to fight nobly in the Battle of the Java Sea; there had been Dutch pilots in Singapore and a few were to fly beside the Allied pilots when the Japanese stormed Java; some, sadly very few, Army officers distinguished themselves. But on the whole the effort was feeble and perhaps this is no better evidenced than by the fact that in the prison camps a wounded Dutchman was a rarity indeed or by the comment of Mr J.J.Jiskoot (at the time of these proceedings

Aerial photograph of the town of Palembang which
straddles the Moesi River.

a sapper and major in the Dutch forces) who says of his
erstwhile contemporary at the Royal Military Academy in
Breda, Colonel Vogelensang (who was in command of the
defence of Palembang): 'My classmate Vogelensang had taken
to his heels with his troops and I blew up the bridge at
Lubukbatang behind his arse.'

So far as the civilians were concerned, an extract from the diary
of the wife of the Deputy District Officer of Palembang is
reasonably typical of their state of mind:

"February 14th. Alert started at 9.00 a.m. Parachutists
landed everywhere. Estimate some 700 of them. News broad-
cast informs us that everything is under control. This does
sound optimistic. Nevertheless, we pack three suitcases for
M.Rudi and myself. Also the silver in a hamper with some food.
Intend to stay in Palembang as long as possible, and with P.
Many desperate people come to P, for advice: whether and how
to get away . . . But he does not know himself what to

recommend, and if they would not get stranded in Tg. Karang [Tandjeonkarang, a port in the southern tip of Sumatra] when fleeing to Java. We intend, if we do have to leave, to go first to Rajoe Agoeng and from there with O's car up country. But we still hope that the British forces will arrive in time to hold Palembang."

Not all the Europeans in Palembang had flight on their minds; there were some who were only too well aware that on the airfield, outnumbered and untrained for such a situation, were beleaguered men. Amongst those in the town were those pilots of 232 and 258 Squadrons who were not on readiness that morning. The 232 pilots did not have quite the same motivation as did those of 258 who (unaware that they had by now been withdrawn to P.2) imagined their friends still on P.1 and felt the urge to give them some sort of hand. I am forever indebted to one of these 258 pilots, another of our Americans, 'Red' Campbell, who while panic raged around him had the consideration to go back to our brothel and collect all the most valuable items left there by pilots then at P.1, included amongst which was my log-book which, possibly uniquely, I managed to keep hidden from the Japanese through three and a half years of captivity. However, before collecting these treasures, Campbell, absolutely in character, made his own attempt to assist us more directly:

"I was in town with 'Ting' Macnamara, Cicurel, Tudor Jones and there was an airman by the name of Peter. I never knew his last name. [In fact it was Lamont.] When they dropped the paratroopers, we tried to get back out to the field. Scotty was there too. And so when they dropped the paratroopers we mobilized and first thing we did was go over and raid the Dutch armoury in town and arm ourselves with rifles. I remember I got myself a rifle and a short Tommy Gun. Not the heavy Thompson but a sort of like little burp gun and we took off. We were going to go out and fight the paratroopers.

"Well we got to a road block. The Japanese had already cut the road off and we got to this road block and we ran into some army and we also ran into a lot of Dutch going the other way. And we decided to set up a sort of line there and see if we couldn't hold. And that was the last time I remember seeing

Pilot Officer 'Ting' Macnamara, the one Rhodesian in 258 Squadron.

Scotty. What happened was I left him to hold a particular position (he had some troops with him there) and 'Ting' Macnamara and myself went off in another direction. We were going to sort of skirt round and see if we could get through to the field. And Ting and I ran into some Dutch Ambonese troops – their native troops. They were showing us the way through and there was some gunfire and we all took cover and I always remember we were lying in a sort of cane brake and we saw these soldiers, looked like Japanese, and Ting, who it turned out was a dead shot, drew a bead on one of them – I drew a bead on the other one and fortunately I missed. Ting didn't. He hit one and it turned out they were Dutch troops, which we found out when we went over to take a look at them.

"But about this time the Japanese did arrive. There were . . . I don't know, about four or five of them. They came out of some brush and to this day I will never know what they had in mind. All they had to do was level their guns and fire and we were mutton! Ting took off in one direction and I, like a damn fool, took off running away from them. They ran after me and for some reason I will never understand they were determined they were going to stick me with a bayonet. They didn't fire their rifles and I was making like John Wayne. I had out a pistol and

I was trying to shoot over my shoulder and hit 'em off at the path. Fortunately some Ambonese soldiers came along about that time and used their short carbines and sabres and waded in and just wiped these Japanese out. I was never so pleased in my life. I went over to take a look because I'd emptied this pistol in their direction and just couldn't believe nothing had happened. I did find a bullet hole in one of the corpses, so I always believed that it was mine. I couldn't believe that I'd missed completely.

"Anyway we realized that we weren't going to get through that way and we came back looking for Scotty. But I guess they'd moved. There was a group of them moved off to another area, then were cut off and ended up walking out to the other side of the island and finished by going to India. I always wished that I had gone in that direction but you do what seems right at the time."

8
Hand to Hand

For all the panic in Palembang, on the airfield things were by no means going as badly as might have been expected. There were not the seven hundred paratroopers believed by the Deputy District Officer's wife but three hundred and sixty of which one hundred, at Pladjoe, had been very badly mauled. Of the two hundred and sixty at P.1 (to whom the jungle posed equal problems as to the defenders) there must have been many casualties both through accident whilst being dropped and through the combined efforts of the ground staff, the air defence men under Creegan and Taute and the noble efforts of the Maréchausée. Also, no doubt, the survivors were by now having to look carefully at their remaining supply of ammunition. They might temporarily have rendered the airfield useless from an operational point of view and they may have destroyed a few vehicles and inflicted many casualties on the defenders, but they had captured no material of consequence and, apart from sporadically cutting the road to the town, had established no important ground positions.

Just as the Japanese at Pladjoe had partially failed in their objective of preventing sabotage to the installations, so were they being foiled at P.1 of seizing supplies of aircraft fuel, and for that matter, aircraft. Taute, (who was to be awarded the Military Cross for his efforts on that day and who it will be recalled had been instructed by Maguire to destroy the petrol dump) set about doing so. The dump was located on the west side of the airfield and was fairly near to a straw-roofed shed containing bombs and ammunition. It was composed of a huge number of forty-four-gallon drums all stacked together and covered with branches:

"Have you ever set fire to a fuel dump? It's not that easy I can tell you. I can tell you what time of day it was. I can tell you because always, like clockwork, every afternoon at about three o'clock, it pissed down with rain. We came marching back along that track to the airfield from the gunpits and it started raining. It doesn't worry you normally because it's warm rain, and it's a warm country, so you just get wet. Anyway we arrived at this fuel dump and apart from my .303 rifle, I had a .38 pistol. Standard issue to officers. And we had some matches. So I sent a man on ahead to report to Maguire at the Headquarters building and I kept one of the sergeants. I think it was Sergeant Moses. A very solid, dependable character. And we stood looking at this dump for a while. I said to him: 'Have you got any matches, Moses?' And he said, yes, he had. So, I said 'Right. Well now, I'll make some holes in the bottoms of the drums and then we'll see if we can set fire to it.' Mind you it was pouring with rain. So I took out this popgun and fired six shots. And it punched neat holes in the bottom of the drums. No trouble. And the petrol came squirting out. And it squirted out into this ditch, which already was full of water. So now you have water with petrol floating on top of it and rain raining on it. And a match to set fire to it. Ha! Ha! Ha! Of course I tried to bend over and shield a match and drop it. You had to watch out – the matches were getting wet as well. And so we couldn't do it. And finally I got Moses to stand astride this trench, facing me, and I straddled the trench facing him. And then we put . . . what do you call those things? A groundsheet! That's it . . . a groundsheet over our heads to keep the rain out.

"Now, we've got the dry matches and the petrol in the trench flowing below us. So I struck a match and I said: 'Moses! When I drop this match, you jump! Uh?' 'Yes, sir.' So I dropped the match and pheeeeeew . . . We didn't have to jump. We were flung right across the road. Yes, into the mud. We were wearing tropical kit. Every hair on our legs was scorched off! My eyebrows had gone! His hat had gone! My hat had gone! But it went up. It went up with a nice big bang. Of course then the petrol that was on the top of the water went up in a sheet of flame. It went through the holes in the drums as well. And they exploded. And the rest of the stuff went up as well. I can tell you, it was quite a bang! We ran like hell. We picked ourselves up and ran. And fortunately, it didn't go all in one big bang. It went in a sort of series of bangs. The bottom drums which had been punched of course went off first and then, I imagine, the heat and flame from them either melted or bent or buckled the petrol in the rest of the drums and it gradually spread. Then we got back to Headquarters. And there was Mac. So he said: 'Oh, well done. I see you set fire to the dump. Well let's see what we can find for you to do next.' "

While the pilots of 232 Squadron played a greater part in the Far East campaign generally than did those of 258 Squadron, this did not apply to Sumatra, largely because 232 operated in greater strength from Singapore. However, some of its pilots and other personnel did have their share of action. The Squadron Operational Record book was lost in the evacuation from Palembang but a record was subsequently written up by the Squadron Adjutant, Flight Lieutenant H.Welch (who escaped to India), from his own personal notebook and with the aid of two pilots who, being unfit for flying duties at the time, had been evacuated with ground personnel.

Pilots on readiness in dispersal. (Author standing.)

On the 14th they lost one pilot, Pilot Officer McCulloch (not to be confused with his namesake in 258 Squadron), who, almost out of petrol, having flown up from Java, was attacked by Zeros and shot down; wounded, he was transferred to Java and subsequently reached Colombo by hospital ship. He was more fortunate than some of the ground personnel. The account reads:

"The Japanese today attacked the aerodrome of Palembang 1 and the Squadron ground personnel were in action. One officer, two senior N.C.O.s and one airman were killed, two missing believed killed and one airman is missing. At the time of the Japanese attack the Squadron Engineering Officer, Flying Officer H.L.Wright with all Flight and Maintenance Personnel was at the aerodrome which lay about ten miles north of the town. The adjutant, Flight Lieutenant N.Welch, the Defence Officer, Pilot Officer J.H.Clough and the Equipment Officer, Pilot Officer B.A.M.Clark, were in the town with the remainder of the Squadron personnel . . . The Japanese did not succeed in capturing the aerodrome itself, but they did cut and hold the only road to the town. It was impossible for the Hurricanes to use the aerodrome as the Japanese had established a considerable air superiority in the neighbourhood and it was decided to work the Hurricanes from Palembang 2 which lay about forty miles to the south-west. The personnel at the aerodrome were ordered to get back to the town and it was in doing this that our casualties occurred. Flying Officer Wright organized a party in one lorry which was mounted with machine guns by the armourers. There were too many men for one lorry so some of the men climbed on a petrol bowser which went on ahead of the lorry. A mile or so down the road they were ambushed and the petrol bowser overturned, blocking the road, trapping and crushing an airman A.C.1 Kilpatrick H. Another airman A.C.2 Duff J.L. sustained a broken leg and probably a broken jaw. He was helped to the side of the road while the remainder of the party laboured to lift the bowser and rescue Kilpatrick. Having no tools or suitable timber, this proved difficult, and before it could be accomplished the Japanese attacked in force. Flying Officer Wright was killed and the rest had to take cover. Nothing more was seen of Duff. Kilpatrick was still alive and subsequently a Corporal Medical

Orderly crawled up under covering fire and injected a double dose of morphia which probably killed him.

"Meanwhile Flight Sergeant Smith J.A. and Sergeant Ratcliffe L. had been sent on ahead in an Army service car used by the 3rd Battery Heavy A.A. There were army personnel in the car as well and this car was ambushed by the Japanese and all its occupants killed. A.C.2 Presdee R.A. was one of a party of unarmed men making their way in single file along the road towards the town. This party was ambushed. He is believed to have lost his life then as nothing more is known of him. L.A.C.Thompson T.E. is a driver M.T. who was on duty at the aerodrome and nothing has been heard of him. Most of the Squadron moved to Palembang 2 for the night of February 14th."

This account is confirmed as reasonably accurate by a letter sent to me more than forty years after the events occurred by G.W.Jones, at the time an armourer with 605 Squadron who wrote:

". . . We never did have breakfast. A bomb had been dropped, a direct hit which gave the lads no chance. At about 2.00 p.m. we looked around and found that personnel were disappearing and decided that it was time that we made a move towards Palembang. A driver brought up a petrol tanker. Three men and the driver were in the cab, two men on the nearest footboard, Norman (Norman Conew – another 605 Squadron armourer) and myself were on the offside footboard and two men between the tank and cab. We set off towards Palembang but after half a mile we ran into trouble: upturned vehicles and men lying in the road. Norman shouted that he had been hit in the foot. I looked down to find that a bullet had lodged between the leather sole and the upper of his shoe. I had just straightened up when the vehicle was hit and swerved and then rolled over towards the left side throwing Norman and myself in the air over the vehicle and crashing down on to the road. We got up and made for the wood at the side of the road for cover. Some of our pals were trapped under the vehicle. We ventured to go into the road to help free them and met with more rifle fire from the Japs. From the injuries that I saw there was no chance of saving their lives.

"We decided to get into the wood and follow the road until we got some help. It was difficult crawling through the four-foot high grass without giving our position away to the snipers. We were also bitten by large red ants. Norman, who was suffering from concussion, kept passing out which meant me dragging him most of the way. I looked down at the front of my shirt which was like a red flag with blood from a large cut under my chin and a cut lip, a V-gap was broken in my front top teeth, my right leg beginning to go stiff because of the impact when landing on the road after the accident. After about another two hours slow progress we were found by a search party from Palembang and taken to a house used as a first aid centre where a Dutch nurse treated my injuries and put four metal clips in my chin wound. I was tired and hungry but by now my jaw had set and I fed by pushing bananas through my broken teeth for four days."

The 'upturned vehicles and personnel lying in the road' to which Mr Jones refers would have been the result of an ambush which had taken place shortly before the petrol bowser arrived and which Hedley Bonnes gives details of in his own account:

". . . Shortly after that they dropped paratroops. I was just down the road. I can't remember whether I was coming up to the aerodrome or going away. But we saw these blasted aircraft coming over and we thought they were Hudsons. I don't know whether they had RAF markings on them. I'm almost certain they had a dish on the side. It could have been the rising sun; it could have been RAF markings. We saw these damn things coming over and, of course, when they started to bale out, I knew they couldn't carry all that crew, so they weren't in trouble – *we* were in trouble! One or two brave lads were popping off. The Dutch had disarmed us the night before, said they required the arms and so forth for their own troops. Said they were very short of arms and that we, as air force, didn't require arms. They'd be protecting us, you see. And rely on our ground defence. But of course it was all this blessed fifth column work. But one or two of these chaps got knocked off and we managed to get a few armaments later this way. Off the dead Japs. And one or two of our chaps weren't very well either, so we got some from them.

"Anyway these parachutes came down and a lot of them came down in the trees and so forth. Well you know the sort of blessed jungle it was. But they had these native chaps, you know, these Dutch native chaps. And I'm almost certain, I stand to be corrected, but they had a sort of chant. It always sounded to me like 'Mah Jongg! Mah Jongg!' And they had a Luger pistol in one hand and a sort of parang in the other. And they would go into the jungle . . . they seemed to be enjoying this and, perfectly true, I saw one chappie there and I thought he'd got a bunch of figs on a piece of string but it wasn't, as God's my judge, they were ears. Ears! I think they got so much an ear, you know. I was only too pleased they were on our side. We did ask one of these Dutch chaps, can we join them? He told us to push off. We were in this stupid light khaki stuff, I mean, and they were all in green camouflage. So we started going down the road. There was a pile up at the end there.

"This is where I can quote from Ted Ravenscroft and Bill Kelly and the chaps who came down in a lorry which had run into a bunch of paratroops which had opened up on them and killed the driver. Ted Ravenscroft got a graze on the head when a bullet came in from the back. Bill Kelly was also in the truck with the driver and the lorry came to a sudden, shuddering stop. Bill Kelly jumped out and was immediately shot in the stomach by a Jap and they took them prisoner. And they forced them into a ditch. On the back of the lorry there were Perks and Broadmoor, and Hall, and another chappie I can't remember. They were wounded in the back, rather badly wounded. And the Japs finished them off . . . which was probably a mercy, really. But although Bill Kelly was shot in the stomach, they managed to get him into this ditch. The Japs stood over them in the ditch debating how to get rid of them. There must have been about eight or nine chaps there and about five Japanese. I suppose they didn't have all that ammunition and didn't want to waste what they had got. But while they were arguing apparently these Ambonese chappies came out of the jungle and knocked them all off while they were trying to make up their minds. So our chaps got out of the ditch and about then I came along. The natives pushed off and things quietened down a bit and we managed to get Bill Kelly and the rest into a lorry and get them away. And we, in turn, got into another truck and pushed off along the road and got back to Palembang."

This story is closely corroborated by Desmond Timmins, at the time a Leading Aircraftman, also of 605 Squadron. He, like others was waiting for breakfast to be cooked, saw the aircraft carrying the paratroops arrive and recognized them as Hudsons. At the same time the accompanying bombers dropped their anti-personnel bombs and as Timmins dived into a slit trench he suddenly felt a 'push in the back' and landed on his face. When the planes had gone, unaware he was quite badly wounded, Timmins scrambled out to find all around him, dead and badly wounded men, while one of the survivors, Leading Aircraftman C.J. ('Tich') Hornsby, seeing blood pouring from Timmins, ripped his shirt off and tied his own first-aid dressing around his body.

Later, after loading the dead and badly wounded into a lorry they set off down the road towards Palembang but after a mile or so the lorry slowed, ran on to the verge and one wheel went into the ditch. In Timmins' words:

"We all finished in a great big heap inside the truck. From what I could gather afterwards, we had run into an ambush of Japanese paratroopers who had blocked the road with cars and

'Des' Timmins. Photograph taken after repatriation.

trucks. I remember them standing at the back of the truck gesturing to us to get out. I had great difficulty getting from underneath the badly injured and dead comrades. As I attempted to jump out of the truck, one of the paratroopers was firing his revolver indiscriminately into it and I can remember the bullets hitting the backboard of the cab. How I dodged them, God only knows.

"They made us all lie in the ditch, half across one another. I remember the thousands of giant red ants which began to crawl all over us and I remember Tich putting the first aid dressing back on the wound on my back, which had slipped down. I think there were about six or seven paratroopers there. The length of time we spent in the ditch could have been ten minutes or half an hour. After a while Tich Hornsby whispered to me to keep my head down and then there was the crack of rifle fire. When we looked up the Japanese paratroopers were lying dead in the road. I am told one of them ran off into the jungle. Out of the tall growth at the back of us, came half a dozen green-uniformed Javanese troops with a Dutch officer, who, I remember, had on green puttees, as worn by our troops in the first world war and there appeared to be a bullet hole through the puttee on one leg. One of the Javanese ran after the paratrooper who had gone off into the jungle and came back later saying he had cut his head off!"

Meanwhile, Timmins also reports, a Bofors gun manned by British troops was pumping shells into the lorries blocking the road and when a passage had been cleared a Dutch armoured truck arrived and transported them to a First Aid Depot on the outskirts of Palembang. From here Timmins was taken to P.2 where he was operated upon before being evacuated to Java where he spent most of the few weeks, prior to his captivity, in a hospital run by nuns.

In his account Timmins confirms the deaths of Perks, Broadmoor and Hall reported by Bonnes. However there was a rather ironic sequel to the death of Hall. The Hall who was killed was confused with another Hall, Bob Hall of 605 Squadron, who escaped injury but whose parents were notified he had lost his life in the Far East. His mother turned his bedroom into a shrine and so it remained until after the war when Hall returned.

On P.1 'Paddy' Creegan (reputed to have been a one-time IRA activist) was having a busy time – as his opposite number, Taute, tells:

"Let's see. What did we do next? Yes. That's right. Down there by the side of the airfield where that Bofors gun was, there was a ditch and running across were some slip trenches. And there were some roughly parallel to the runway. And in them were seven or eight Japanese who'd come running out of the jungle and got into them. And these trenches were at right angles to the ditch. Quite a deep ditch. I suppose it was a natural watercourse or something. And they started shooting at us. From these slip trenches. And so Maguire decided they were a bit of a nuisance. We shouldn't allow this. And so Paddy Creegan put on his tin hat and took a rifle and decided that he'd crawl down and shoot these fellows from the side. Enfilade them as it were. So Paddy went down into the ditch on all fours, dragging his rifle, and he'd hardly got a little way when the Dutchmen in the Bofors gun emplacement started shooting at him. I suppose they thought he was a Japanese. It's not easy to tell, you know. Anybody wearing some sort of khaki which is covered by mud and everything else by now. So they see this fellow crawling in the ditch with a rifle. And I suppose in their simple minds they thought: there's a fellow, he shouldn't be crawling along, obviously up to no good . . . So they started shooting at him. Paddy went down on his face in such a hurry that his tin hat nearly broke his nose. Hit him right across the nose. He was pouring with blood. He turned back and came back to the Headquarters building, cursing these Dutchmen. But then, I don't know quite why, these Japs suddenly came out of this trench and started running and it happened that Maguire and I each had a rifle and we knocked off three or four of them before they could get back into the jungle. Well then there was peace and quiet after that so we could sit down and discuss what's to do . . ."

It is convenient to pick up Maguire's own account at this point:

"At this time we were settling down. Enemy fire was not heavy, harassing I suppose was the term one could use, but our side seemed fairly well protected and we settled down, in effect to wait. We were in fact feeling fairly confident that we could repel the sort of attack that we could foresee. However about four o'clock a Hurricane flew over and dropped a message which told us that a further Japanese landing in some considerable force was taking place on a river some fifteen miles north of us and told us, in effect, to evacuate. As a result of this we had a Council of War and Creegan and I thought it might be sensible to do a short recce alongside the road leading to Palembang to see what chance we had of getting lorries down the road. We passed the word to the others to stay under cover but be ready for a quick loading operation. We spoke to the Maréchausée Dutch people who looked at us fairly blankly and I think rather lost confidence in us, possibly through poor communication. There had been no fire from the road area for some time past. Most of it was two or three hundred yards to the east and Creegan and I picked our way, creeping through the rubber going up the hill towards Palembang. As we reached the top of the slight incline, we saw a Japanese soldier bending over a machine gun, I think he was putting it in position to enfilade the road, but I don't think he was ready to fire it. He stood up and saw us at a range of about fifty yards. Although we were both armed we had Thompson machine guns and I had no confidence in the ability of these weapons to reach him in time. So, telling Creegan we would have to bluff it out, I laid down my unwieldy weapon and marched briskly up to him. He looked very surprised but did nothing. So, sounding as confident as I could, I demanded to see his officer and, to my amazement, he shambled off and produced an officer, a Captain I would say, although at the time I wasn't observing rank very closely. This officer had some command of English and I immediately demanded surrender saying that I had a large force behind me. He replied that he had a large force and that he would give us safe conduct if we marched out. This indeed we both doubted and I then said I would have to go back and report to my superiors and see what should be done. And again turning round, with quite a number of qualms, we marched briskly down the road, picked up our weapons and rejoined our own lines.

Here we debated whether we should stick it out in view of the fact we had been told to evacuate. We felt that by going forward a surprise dash by lorries would not be very productive and we decided firstly to destroy what equipment was left around the airfield that we could get at, to offer the Dutch soldiers a bit, if they wished it, and to tell them about the increasing threat from the north once again. Although there were divided councils as to whether it would be advisable to try the western route eventually this was agreed and we destroyed what we could, loaded up (we had a couple of slightly wounded) and headed off our three lorries to the north of the airfield.

The Maréchausée, I think, had wisely reckoned they had done what they could and would blend more easily into the native population. They were mostly Achinese and melted is the word into the surrounding bush and did not wish to come with us. I am not exactly certain – I think we had three truckloads and there were about sixty or eighty of us altogether."

The remarkable episode of the parley between Maguire and the Japanese, which enabled a substantial body of men to escape unscathed who would otherwise probably have suffered severe casualties, has now established itself in the annals of legend. Like all legends there are many versions with each version differing considerably from its neighbour. I gave my own version in *Hurricane Over the Jungle*. It was a treasured recollection carried in my memory for nearly forty years. I do not know whether I heard my version second-hand or whether it was the residue of the story which Maguire himself may have told me when we ended up in the same prison camp in Java. In fact my own version is by no means so crashingly at variance with truth as many of the accounts which have been offered to me. This by no means indicates that the story has been deliberately exaggerated or falsified. Nor even does it mean that men who categorically state they were present at the parley, and clearly could not have been, were lying. The mind is a strange vehicle which gathers together happenings, rumours and aspirations and simmers them over the years. The product which is finally established has been conditioned by attitude and emotion and as such is usually one to suit the make-up of its owner. Over the years, unchallenged, by a process of auto-suggestion, romanticism often becomes reality, myth becomes historical fact and enthusiasm experience.

9
The P.2 Effort

I am indebted to Group Captain Plenty for information as to the general situation at P.2 on 14 February.

Just after 11 a.m. Group Captain McCauley, the Station Commander, was advised of the paratroop landings at P.1 by the AOC (Air Commodore Hunter) who informed him, incorrectly, that the airfield was being evacuated and he must be ready for a similar evacuation at P.2. Some time later the actual order to evacuate came through together with an order to fly all serviceable aircraft to Batavia. McCauley accordingly started the machinery for demolition, denial and evacuation; all secret and confidential files and publications were destroyed; equipment, stores and rations were collected for disposal; and approximately twenty Hudsons were loaded with personnel and equipment and dispatched to Java. That such large numbers of RAF and RAAF personnel on this vast and rambling airfield should be hastily rushing here, there and everywhere in the steamy Sumatran heat, destroying or preparing to destroy practically everything in sight on an airfield the Japanese did not even know existed and which was in any case some forty or fifty miles from the nearest one of them, gives some indication of the panic which had gripped Palembang.

Not long after this destruction had been put in hand, a number of officers from Group Headquarters in the town, having already burnt and destroyed everything there, arrived at P.2 only to learn quite soon that not only were the total number of paratroops which had been dropped less than four hundred, but that they were being held. An attempt was made to put everything into reverse, orders were given for the aircraft which had been sent down to Batavia to return, and the officers set off back to their Headquarters.

However, as may be imagined, all these orders and counter-orders hardly improved the operational efficiency of the rump of the squadrons still remaining the more so as, through a further breakdown in communications, the order instructing the Hudsons to return was not received in Java. The only fortunate thing was that the disposal of bombs, fuel and ammunition had been left to the last and their destruction had not yet taken place.

Unserviceable aircraft had been included in the destruction order but now attempts were made to repair two of such machines – one with a crushed fuselage and the other without an engine. Although few facilities remained, the squadron personnel set to work and by nightfall had fitted a new aileron to the former and work was in hand to reinstall the engine which had been removed from the latter. Flight Sgt Musica, in charge of this operation, worked with a bayonet and some tools taken from a steamroller and by dawn of the 15th the engine was back in place. Meanwhile the heavy anti-aircraft guns, which of course were serving no useful purpose, were used to create a road block about a mile north of the station and machine-gun and rifle parties placed to combat any Japanese attempt to seize the airfield.

Prior to all these panic instructions being received, P.2 had been a reasonably efficient station geared up to doing what it could with its limited, but useful, resources to blunt the Japanese invasion.

The Japanese convoys which the reconnaissance Hudsons from P.2 had sighted on the previous day, had joined together on the night of 13/14 February and on the latter were discovered heading for the mouth of the Moesi River. There are discrepancies in opinions as to the make-up of this convoy. In the official Royal Australian Air Force history section records compiled by W.R.Lyster in 1946, the force was reported as consisting of one battleship, three or four cruisers, seven destroyers and between twenty-five and thirty transports with 'an aircraft carrier (*Ryuko*) sheltering near Banka Island'. David Thomas in his excellent *Battle of the Java Sea* suggests six cruisers *Chokai, Kumano, Suzuya, Mikuma, Mogami* and *Yura* , eleven destroyers, the aircraft carrier *Ryuko*, five minesweepers, two submarine chasers and twenty-five transports plus other 'screening warships'. But whatever the exact make-up was, it is undeniable that a massive target awaited the attentions of the bombers on P.2.

It will be recalled that the units based on P.2 consisted of the Australian Nos 1 and 8 Squadrons and a mixed bag of RAF echelons including No 84 Squadron. In general terms Mr Lyster's records concentrate on the efforts of the Australian squadrons. The records state:

"Five Hudsons from No. 8 Squadron departed from P.2 at 0500 hours for an offensive patrol off Banka Island but one pilot touched the ground just after the aircraft was airborne and the undercarriage had been raised, with the result that ten inches were shorn off each propeller blade. The pilot however managed to keep the aircraft in the air until first light, when it landed at P.1.

"Two Hudsons, whose captains were Flt. Lts. Marshall and Plenty, proceeded to attack warships off the north of Banka Island. All their bombs were near misses. Another aircraft attacked enemy transports near Panjaran Island but the bombs failed to release. The captain of this aircraft, Flt. Lt. Maynard, carried out a reconnaissance of South Muntok and then proceeded to Lahat as there was an air raid in progress at P.1.

"No. 1 Squadron aircraft took off in three waves, all in search of different targets as given them by the Operations Room but they all attacked the Japanese convoy proceeding towards the Moesi River which was steaming in two parallel lines.

"On their way to the target all three formations were attacked by enemy fighters over the town of Palembang but these they managed to evade. Again when about ten miles from the target they were attacked by formations of Navy '0's with a top cover of M.E.109s. [This does seem unlikely!] By making use of cloud cover, the Hudsons again escaped and reached the target which they proceeded to attack. During this attack the first two flights of Hudsons, each of three aircraft, were again beset by Navy '0's. Flt. Lt. J.K.Douglas carried out a dive attack after leading his flight to the target in cloud which he dived through down sun. He climbed back into the clouds and subsequently delivered another attack, but this time his aircraft was seen to burst into flames and dived into the sea. Flt. Lt. T.J.O'Brien, who was in the same flight, scored three direct hits on the transport that he selected and it fell out of line listing to starboard. The gunner later saw it on fire.

"In the second flight of No. 1 Squadron Hudsons, Flt. Lt. O.N.Diamond scored two direct hits on the stern of a M.V, Flt. Lt. A.J.L.Williams scored one direct hit on the stern of another and Flt. Lt. A.H.Brydon scored two direct hits and one near miss on yet another M.V. During his attack Flt. Lt. Diamond was chased by two Navy '0's who fired on him continuously and succeeded in putting his starboard engine out of action, shot away his starboard landing wheel and badly damaged his empennage unit. With full throttle on the port engine and one hundred feet above the water he made his way to the mouth of the Moesi River in an endeavour to reach P.1. He did manage to get there, where he made a crash landing. He then discovered that the aerodrome was surrounded by Japanese paratroopers who had landed about an hour previously. Amid rifle and tommy-gun fire Flt. Lt. Diamond led his crew, who were all uninjured, towards a Mark III Hudson standing on the runway. This was the No. 8 Squadron aircraft which had been abandoned earlier with the tips missing from its propeller blades. Flt. Lt. Diamond started up this machine and attempted to take off but he could not get above 40 knots and ground-looped it. After a hurried look round at some Hurricanes and Buffalos, which turned out to be U/S, he led his crew off into the surrounding paddy fields pursued by Japanese with hand grenades. After crawling through the paddy fields (which they were sharing with leeches and various insects) for ten hours, they got past the Japanese and, joining up with a small body of Allied troops, made their way to Palembang and returned to P.2 on 15 February.

"Flt. Lt. Brydon's aircraft was also badly damaged by machine gun bullets and shrapnel but managed to make P.2.

"The third flight of Hudsons consisted of two aircraft from No. 1 Squadron flying in company with three Hudsons from 62 Squadron. These five aircraft proceeded up the coast to the Bintang Hari River and then on a course of 060 degrees to the target. But soon after sighting it they were attacked by a squadron of Navy '0's. The two aircraft of No. 1 Squadron pressed on and both simultaneously dived on separate ships. Flt. Lt. J.A.Lockwood was immediately afterwards seen to be losing height with smoke issuing from one of his engines and with two Navy '0's on his tail. Flg. Off. P.J.Gibbes, who was the captain of the only survivor of the five aircraft, scored a direct hit on a M.V. The three Hudsons from 62 Squadron were apparently destroyed before they reached the target."

The effort from P.2 was, however, far from concluded as will be seen as we turn our attention to the events on the following day.

10
The Second Day

By the time dawn broke on Sunday, 15 February, the Dutch had abandoned all thoughts of holding Sumatra. To put this fact into proper perspective a few comparisons may be useful. Sumatra, a fiercely inhospitable country, largely without roads or railways, clothed in vast mountains, miasmal swamps and horrendous jungle, slashed by wide, torrential rivers, subjected daily to violent downpours, a breeding ground for tropical diseases and swarming with dangerous insects, animals and reptiles, has an area of 170,000 square miles. This is almost twice the combined areas of another inhospitable group of countries: Vietnam, Cambodia and Laos. It is thirteen times the area of its then mother country, Holland. It is greater in area than the second largest of America's states, California. Greater in area than Italy, Yugoslavia, Poland or East and West Germany combined; almost as large as Spain or France. It is considerably larger than its conqueror, Japan. Yet within twenty-four hours this huge, forbidding and immensely rich territory had accepted defeat at the hands of a small, mauled group of paratroopers and a river-borne force which had yet to reach the outskirts of a single, if important, town.

When one recalls the manner in which on tiny islands small forces of Japanese after weeks of saturation bombing and shelling, without the least air or sea support, resisted for weeks on end reoccupying forces outnumbering them ten to one and more, it is a sobering thought.

Flight from the Japanese had begun. Palembang's Deputy District Officer's wife wrote in her diary: 'At 4.00 a.m. the resident phones to tell us that all women and children should leave immediately. Many had already left . . . The telephone was ringing without stop. At 5.30 a.m. M wakes me up. We have to get dressed immediately as Beppie O is on her way with the car and the three children. No time even to wash or brush my hair. Suitcases shut . . . '

Already the ferry across the Moesi was choked with cars and lorries, their owners (with the port of Oosthaven on Sumatra's southern tip a beckoning gateway to Java and escape from the terrible Japanese) importuning, bribing, threatening, pleading for priority. At Padang on the west coast, more than three hundred miles distant, on the other side of a high mountain range, hasty preparations for departure were in hand. Even on the far-away northern tip, at Koetaradja, no less than eight hundred and fifty miles away by direct aircraft flight and probably not much less than twelve hundred miles by road, the British Vice-Consul was to write of 15 February to the Secretary of State in London: 'The last of the regular troops in the coastal areas has been transferred inland to Prapat on the shores of Lake Toba [some seventy miles away].'

Rumour and despair were everywhere. There was the sense that at any instant Japanese would miraculously debouch from behind the nearest bush. Communication, primitive enough at the best of times, was rapidly breaking down altogether. Orders and counter-orders confused even those who still retained the will to resist. While command, theoretically, lay with the Dutch, such practical opposition as might be mounted, could only come from the Americans, Australians, British and New Zealanders who made up the Air Force Squadrons and the Anti-Aircraft Batteries.

Yet down in the south, at Oosthaven, had been landed, or were about to land, a sufficient number of troops which properly disposed, properly led, might well have been strong enough to throw the invaders into the Moesi which was in any case to be littered with their dead before the day was through. These forces comprised a light tank squadron of the 3rd Hussars which had been disembarked on the previous day and 3,400 Australians including the 2/3rd Machine Gun Battalion and the 2/2 Pioneer Battalion due to disembark on the 15th from the *Orcades*. Had such a force already been established in the Palembang area, the Japanese, facing all the problems of terrain, supply and disease might have been hard-pressed. Had the initial invasion failed, valuable time would have been bought and the invasion of Java might never have occurred for there is little doubt that the capture of Southern Sumatra with its airfield of P.1 was a necessary precursor. Even more galling is the fact that documentation was subsequently to show that it had for some time been appreciated that the attack on Sumatra would almost certainly be mounted on the Palembang area and that the method of attack would be precisely that which, in the event, the Japanese employed – by parachute and barge.

Before recounting the local events of this memorable and fascinating day, we should perhaps pause and spare space and thought for those other, rather more distant actors who play their part in this account – Major Donald Wright in the *Hung Jow* originally intended to carry thirteen men to Java, now loaded down to its gunwales with wounded from the sunk merchant vessel and Puckridge magically picked up from his 'Lilo' at dead of night in the open Southern China Sea; Brigadier Bird on Motor Launch *M.L.433* who had entered the Banka Strait the previous night; Flight Lieutenant 'Denny' Sharp seeking a way to rejoin his squadron; and a newcomer to the list the *Mary Rose* leaving Singapore only hours before the island fell, transporting amongst about one hundred and fifty others, one Frank Brewer, CMG, OBE, and a Mr Bowden, the Australian Trade Commissioner in Singapore.

Donald Wright, who it will be recalled was now, following a change of plan, hoping to find a hospital somewhere up the Inderagriri River where they might off-load their wounded passengers reports of the 15th.

"We passed some fishing villages at the mouth of the Inderagiri River, most picturesque villages, with all the houses on stilts, and eventually we managed to persuade a local fisherman to come on board and guide us up. The Inderagiri, incidentally, is quite a wide river but it is very difficult because it is extremely fast-flowing and full of sandbanks and mud-

Sumatran home for sixteen families with communal
burying place in foreground.

banks. This good fellow took us up the river for some sixty miles
until we came to a tiny village called Latjow. This was on
midday February 15th. At this time we had no idea where the
Japs were, so a small party of us was landed while the
remainder went on up the river.

"We found out that there were no Japs nearby and so
managed to get another launch and join the main party at a
village called Tambilaham thirty miles further up the river. It
was here that we learned that the Japs were already in
possession of Palembang to the south and we had no idea
whether they might move north or whether they might be on
their way up this very river any moment. We also heard that a
number of ships with escapers on board had been sunk amongst
the islands. There were a number of RNVR other ranks and
officers with us and they immediately took whatever boats they
could find and set off to see if they could give any assistance to
the poor chaps who were stranded on the islands. This was a
very brave gesture as they had no defence at all and they knew
that the Japanese might be after them any moment. Anyhow I

gather that some of them were successful and did manage to bring some survivors back to Sumatra."

Brigadier Bird was having a far less uneventful journey. Having entered the Banka Strait on the night of 14th, he awoke next morning just as it was getting light and saw on the port bow what they all assumed to be Dutch destroyers sent to escort them down to Java. So the Captain, Volunteer Reserve Officer, Commander Campey, hoisted a large White Ensign and no sooner had he done this than there was a swish and a couple of shells from one of the destroyers hissed over the top of them and one landed short and the next salvo landed plumb on the six-pounder gun into, Bird believes, the forward cabin where all the troops were. The Captain gave the order to abandon ship (which merely involved stepping into the water) but Bird believes other officers or troops tried to lower a dinghy because Japanese machine-gun bullets started 'flipping all over the place'. Bird found himself swimming with two men named Smith and Ryan just behind him. Ryan called out that he was a bad swimmer and just then a shark went by about six yards behind him, there was a cry and then a silence which left Bird in no doubt the shark had taken him. Bird splashed 'to no mean purpose' as he'd heard this was the thing to do and then swam over to one of the destroyers and shouted to one of the Japanese on board to throw him a rope – a request which produced much mirth but nothing else. So he swam on and was finally picked up by a Japanese cutter and taken back to his own launch which had not sunk after all, but was down by its bow with its stern up in the air. He was allowed to get on board where he collected a pair of shorts (he'd kicked off his clothes) from his suitcase on deck and, he thinks, a shirt. There was a dinghy on the launch and a Japanese midshipman ordered all who were left there to get into it, cramming it with as many men as it would take but leaving Bird and two other ranks uncatered for. So Bird asked the midshipman to take him back to his destroyer and they were, in fact, allowed to get into the cutter, but when they got near the destroyer a lot of flag-wagging went on, with the upshot that the midshipman (who spoke English) said: 'Sorry. This is war. Out you get.' Bird remonstrated but a Japanese sailor threatened that if he didn't get out he would hit him over head with an oar! So out got the three of them and clambered on to a Carley float which happened to be drifting nearby and there they sat all day.

The *Mary Rose* meanwhile was only now setting out from Singapore. Included in its complement was a party of six men: Brewer, one-time Malayan Civil Servant, who became a member of a special force which came to be known as 'Force 101' which seems mainly to have been concerned with training Chinese Communists for jungle warfare against the Japanese; Colonel Dalley, head of the Malayan Police Force Special Branch, who'd been organizing much the same sort of thing; Captain Hawkins, a World War I veteran; two planters, respectively Captain Donald Farquharson and Captain Herring, and a third planter, Lieutenant Eno, who'd come over from Sumatra to join this mysterious Force 101. The idea was that these six men should make their way to Sumatra, find a Colonel Warren of the Royal Marines (who was in Sumatra trying to organize some behind-the-lines units) and offer him their services. Authorization was given to this party to request a Captain Muloch (reputed to have been one of the midshipmen on the expedition to the South Pole to relieve Scott and therefore a man of advanced age) to provide them with a launch. And indeed Muloch did find them a launch, the *Osprey*, in which they set off but only after fending off deserters who: 'threatened us with their tommy-guns and things and even went as far as to chuck grenades at us which, unfortunately for them or fortunately for us, exploded in the water and did no harm'.

They finally set off only to foul their anchor on a buoy and, being unable to disentangle it, transferred to the *Mary Rose* which for all that it had one hundred and fifty on board (one of whom was this Australian civilian, Bowden) was quite a small launch and so jam-packed. They proceeded to sail through a veritable armada of tiny boats each of which held two Japanese who, being busy landing on some new corner of Singapore, took not the least notice of them and in due course, clearing Singapore, they sailed through the islands and at nightfall anchored relieved at, as they believed, making their escape. The next day Muloch, resisting suggestions from Dalley they should head straight for Sumatra and the Inderagiri River, pressed on southwards, sailing through the following night and just before dawn ran directly into the Japanese fleet. As in other cases a Japanese naval officer, acting very correctly, accepted Captain Muloch's surrender, taking his sword, and ordered them all to Muntok. Here, handed over to the care of the Japanese army, they were ordered to empty out their kitbags and so on and from Brewer's fell a small oil bottle. Bowden, who had some knowledge of Japanese, tried to explain to a suspicious soldier that this was merely a harmless item and was promptly beaten about the face. Thereupon Bowden endeavoured to argue his diplomatic status, was beaten up again, then taken outside, forced to dig his own grave and promptly shot.

Mention has been made of the attempts to persuade Air Vice-Marshal Pulford to leave Singapore aboard one of the Lock-

Air Vice-Marshal Pulford meeting Dutch pilots in Singapore.

heed Hudsons flown up from P.2 specifically to collect him and of how he refused to leave what he considered to be his post. He was, however, eventually persuaded to attempt to escape imprisonment and once more I must express my gratitude to Denis Russell-Roberts for supplying me with the fullest details of this attempt and its tragic conclusion. As the story is superbly covered in *Spotlight on Singapore*, I will merely paraphrase it here.

Pulford, as Air Officer Commanding Far East, had been from the outbreak of the Pacific War, General Percival's right-hand man while Rear Admiral Spooner, who was to accompany him, had commanded all Allied naval forces in Malayan waters. They quitted Singapore on 14 February on HM Motor Launch *310* commanded by an RNVR New Zealander, Lieutenant 'Johnny' Bull, DSC, together with five further officers, twelve crew, twenty-seven British soldiers and sailors and a Chinese cook. After the usual problems in getting clear of Singapore things went well enough until approaching the Banka Strait they ran across two Japanese cruisers and two destroyers, supported by five seaplanes. By fierce manœuvring Bull managed to avoid damage both from bombing and gunfire and sought safety off the south-eastern tip of an island called Tjibea where he had decided to beach the launch. He had successfully landed his passengers, including Pulford and Spooner, when a fifth Japanese vessel, a destroyer, approached, closed and opened fire. Bull now instructed his crew to abandon ship and take cover ashore, which they did, while the destroyer ceased fire, closed further and lowered a motor boat manned with heavily armed officers and men which came alongside *310* and accepted the surrender of those remaining on board, Bull, Lieutenant Henderson of the Australian RNVR, Wing Commander Atkins, RAF, and Lieutenant Pool, RN.

The Japanese proceeded to destroy all electrical and wireless fittings, ordered the officers to take to their small dinghy and go ashore, and then returned to their ship. The following morning a Japanese seaplane bombed and strafed *310*, interrupting an attempt being made to make her seaworthy and putting her finally out of commission.

Rear Admiral Spooner now took charge of the party on Tjibea and, assisted by the island's Commandant and aide, two

English-speaking Javanese, set about restoring a native sailing craft, a *prahu*, discovered on the beach, with the idea that a small party would sail in her to Java and fetch assistance. When the craft was ready, Bull set sail accompanied by the two Javanese and two crew members, his coxswain Leading Seaman Brough and Able Seaman Hill, the entire party dressed in native dress to allay suspicions of any Japanese who might observe them. After an arduous passage lasting seven days, surviving sweltering heat and tropical storms, Bull finally succeeded in reaching his destination and alerting the authorities as to the plight of Pulford, Spooner and the others.

Meanwhile, on Tjibea, Spooner was directing the reconditioning of a second derelict native craft but before it could be made seaworthy many of the party had already died from malaria, dysentery, exposure and malnutrition. Amongst those to succumb were Spooner himself, followed shortly afterwards by Pulford. Finally Wing Commander Atkins piloted the survivors in the repaired *prahu* only to encounter a Japanese warship and for all those aboard to be taken prisoner. Of the original party on *310*, fifteen died on Tjebia while two more went missing; another man died within a few days of leaving the island.

In fact an attempt had been made to rescue the escapers. Submarine *S-39* of the US Navy commanded by Lieutenant 'Red' Coe was instructed to make for Tjebia and collect them. According to the submarine's report they located Tjebia on 27 February. That night, and the succeeding night, manœuvring close in, they signalled to the party. On the third night, having obtained no response, a party was sent ashore. In spite of a thorough search of the island (which was a mere one mile long and half a mile wide) they found no signs of life, the only evidence of occupation being recently destroyed native huts and cooking utensils and footprints which, from their size, they judged to be of Japanese origin. Assuming that either the Japanese had landed and taken the party prisoner or alternatively that the party had made their own escape ahead of the Japanese landing, *S-39* withdrew. Whilst it is possible that Coe was in error in believing the island at which he landed was Tjebia, it is, of course, probable that the dead would have been buried by the survivors before they set off on that last futile attempt to avoid imprisonment.

While these dreadful things were occurring, Flight Lieutenant Sharp, continuing his attempt to rejoin his squadron, was, after an unforgettable day which had not been without its problems, enjoying companionship and sustenance in a delightful small hotel far away on the west coast of Sumatra.

"Next morning (February 15th) I moped around and I got hold of this taxi with some assistance from the Dutch Authority – when I say the Dutch Authority, I mean the Dutch civilians who were in this little town, and we engaged this taxi to drive us south to Palembang. We loaded all the machine guns, eight of them which I had stripped from my Hurricane on Singkep and carted across with me to Sumatra, my parachute and harness and all that sort of gear and away we set off for Palembang.

"We'd only driven about two miles when some Dutch farming blokes stopped us standing up, in the middle of the street. 'You can't go any further!' They were speaking in Dutch to start off with but they also could speak English. 'You can't go any further.' 'Why?' 'Because we've sabotaged the oil line which runs along the side of the road and we've set fire to the oil, and the jungle on both sides is alight and there's no way you'll be able to get through.' 'Why have you done this?' 'Well, we have news that Palembang airport has been taken by the Japanese and that foretells that Sumatra is going to fall too.' So they're doing a scorched earth. And that was all about it. We then had to retrace our steps back to Djambi and when we got there out came the maps, out came the advice from the Dutch and when they knew that our destination was Java they said: 'Well you can go down this road and you can eventually get out to the south-west coast and you may be able to pick up some shipping from there. If not you may be able to pick up a suitable boat which will take you down to Java.'

"Okay we opted for that, into the taxi again and away we went. About ten miles out from Djambi we came across a nice little *chong*, creek, river, small river. So we stopped on the middle of the bridge and we off-loaded all the surplus weight now, all the damn machine guns. I had no ammunition because I'd shot that all off to lighten the plane before landing at Singkep. We dropped all these machine guns into the water

A typical rural scene in lowland rice-growing area.

hoping that nobody would ever know they were there and if they did ever find them they wouldn't be any use anyway. So we continued on and after quite a few hours on the road we came to a crossroad and it was a road that was going north from Palembang, in a north-westerly direction towards Padang and funnily enough we met up with I'm not sure if it was one or two, but we met up with at least one truck full of airmen and I'm not quite sure again because it was such a brief visit, I think it was in command of a Royal Air Force Wing Commander. He said he was going to Padang and we said we're not going to Padang, we're going to Bencoolen. So he went his way and we went ours. So on we go.

"We were, at least I was, running short of money at this particular stage. I don't know what I was spending it on but I couldn't have got enough from the first chap. So as we were passing through this Dutch provincial village with a Governor, I called in there and was able to get some more guilders and when I came out and walked down to the car (it was in the village) I met up with a little bit of resistance from the locals. Apparently the driver who knew where we were going, because we'd already told him to drive to Bencoolen, didn't want to go any further because he was getting away from his family and his environment and all that sort of stuff and he was causing a little bit of trouble with the local neighbours. And the local neighbours were on his side. So at this particular stage we had difficulty getting petrol but I was able to convince somebody to get us some petrol and we got the petrol. He needed the petrol to get back anyway . . . Well anyway we got the petrol and then he needed a bit of convincing that he must come with us to Bencoolen. So we got to the stage where the crowd got a wee bit hostile and I had to sort of threaten the crowd by drawing my revolver and saying: 'Stand back! Stand back!' They understood the revolver. They couldn't understand the English, but the driver understood the threatening gestures of getting into the taxi, so he got into the taxi and away we went.

"Things are a bit vague at this stage because I don't know if we stopped anywhere that night or drove all the way to Bencoolen. I can't remember stopping anywhere; the one big thing I do remember is that we had to pass over these hills which are quite high and the driver wasn't very experienced and he had never driven on hills before and as we were starting to come down the other side . . . it was all right going up, but when we started to go down the other side of the hill he just didn't have a clue how to slow up to take the corners. Because the way the vehicle was accelerating its speed he just didn't know what to do. So after a couple of hair-raising corners, I had to tell him to get out of the driving seat and I'd drive for him. He didn't mind at all. So there we were and I was driving from then on down to Bencoolen.

"We arrived at Bencoolen a bit late on the fifteenth of February and after finding out a little bit of information, I rang the Wing Commander who was up in Padang and he told me that a tramp steamer was expected in that day to pick up troops on the way to Batavia and he would ring back and let me know what the score was. At the same time at this hotel I joined up with some Dutch planters and oil workers who had been called up into their army as conscripts or volunteers or whatever you like, and we were sitting around having a few beers and discussing what the position was and all this and they didn't know exactly what to do but they decided that to have a conference at a little Dutch village which was inland about five miles, next morning. And there we were; we went to bed that night in this lovely little hotel after a few cold beers on the arrangement that next day I'd go along with them, not because they wanted me, it was because the bloke, the Dutch fellow, who owned a Chev, a very late model Chev, couldn't drive. He had a native driver who had sort of skipped and there he was stuck with this Chev. So that's why I was going too."

Maguire, meanwhile, with Creegan, Taute and the sixty or seventy men he had spirited away from the Japanese, was also heading for the coast.

"Our general plan on that first evening – we lacked all major maps of Sumatra except one or two air maps which were not as good as surface maps would have been – the general idea was to do a wide left-hand circuit and cut back to P.2 by crossing the river at a more western area. About seven or eight miles to the west of the airfield there was a large rubber plantation and we pulled up to see if we could get some local knowledge from the manager. The manager and his family naturally, having heard the noise of battle from a distance, were in some state of anxiety and delighted to see us and gave us all the information which they had. We told them about the landings and that they should move out and they said they would be delighted to use us as an escort. We were also told that there was a major petrol dump in the rubber some distance from their plantation house. There was a problem in that there was a native *kampong* quite close to this petrol dump but we tracked down the head man, explained the situation and eventually put a match to a couple of million gallons of aircraft fuel which we reckoned there was no sensible reason to leave the Japanese to find. We were also told at this stage that the nearest western road which would bring us back to P.2 would necessitate a considerable drive to the west and then a very large loop south. We had decided that as we had made our presence felt geographically by the fire, we had better set off for a good part of that first night.

"We reached a palm oil estate whose factory manager was

extremely on the ball. He had prepared his people for a pull out if necessary and paid all of his staff and his workers and he was all set to put a match to the assets. He had either a working telephone or a point-to-point radio, I forget which. At any rate, he assured us that the southern road had been cut by the Japanese or was about to be cut according to his information. He also told us that some of the ferries had been destroyed in panic and that we would have to stay on the right hand bank, the northern bank, of the Moesi for some considerable time. In fact on departure we found a ferry that was working and had a fairly uneventful day's trekking west. We pulled in to another *kampong* where the natives were extremely hostile to the point where we kept a very sharp eye on their doings. We left early and as it had been wet in the night I purchased one of these oiled paper umbrellas, dark green in colour, which I think then cost about twenty cents. I then thought that they would make good camouflage so we bought the whole stock at the shop and these sunshades, umbrellas, were issued to each truck with orders to put them up if aircraft sight or sound should occur. I don't know how effective this ploy was, but we certainly did use

A typical Sumatran village meeting house.

them two or three times in this role and were certainly not attacked. This may have just been good fortune.

"We reached the north/south road junction about a day later. We were told at a local police post that shipping had ceased at Padang and that their information was that the road south was cut. Afterwards I had reason to believe that both these statements were wrong. But there was a considerable amount of confusion and rumour. After some discussion we decided that we would head west to Bencoolen, which was apparently still receiving shipping, and was fairly well away from any Japanese advance. On this part of the journey, I remember vividly the beauty of the mountains, the savannahs and a general air of peace and although the area was very thinly populated, it struck me at the time that it would sooner or later become a great asset in eventual development.

"Three or four miles from Bencoolen, we set up a rearguard to delay or stop any Japanese who might appear. We were quite well armed, the road was a ravine and our people were of high morale.

"When I went into the town and sought out the authority, I believe a High Commissioner, he was aghast that we proposed to oppose the Japanese and was all for the quiet life. He told me that he was sure the Japanese would leave the Dutch administration in place and he didn't want them upset. I said my ambition was to get out of Bencoolen as fast as possible and could ships be summoned? He told me that all radio sets had been destroyed. However after a while, with help from the local police and our own people, who had several radio experts, we found and operated a set which got through to, I think, Tjilatjap. At any rate we found a coaster, a small coaster, was due in twenty-four hours and we waited. By this time several of the local Dutch had changed their mind about waiting for the Japanese and had decided to come with us."

It is perhaps pertinent at this stage to enquire what had happened to the Allied fleet which had been assembled under the command of Admiral Doorman for the purpose of impeding the invasion. In fact it had passed through the Sunda Strait on the night of 14/15 February losing one of its destroyers, the *Van Ghent* (which struck a reef) in the process and heading on a

HMS *Exeter* fighting off air attacks in Banka Strait.

north-easterly course with the avowed intention of circling round Banka Island and striking the Japanese invasion force in the rear.

However, the Japanese admiral, Ozawa, fully aware of this threat, organized for continual high-level bombing attacks to be carried out on Doorman throughout daylight on 15 February.

In fact Japanese high-level bombing attacks on moving targets were on the whole rather ineffective due to the rigid formula adopted and the rigid discipline which ensured this formula was strictly adhered to. The system of bombing on Singapore was for groups of aircraft, almost invariably numbering twenty-seven machines, always in perfect formation, to release their bombs simultaneously on instructions from their leader; even though it was clear one's own airfield was about to be attacked, one was able to watch the raiders approaching without undue alarm, knowing that when the whistle of the falling bombs was heard there would be ample time to get down into a slit trench (in which one would have been extraordinarily unlucky to be hurt) and that after the brief thudding (which never extended for more than a few seconds), after this was over one could get out again and feel reasonably confident of not being bothered any more that day.

Being attacked at sea was a much more nerve-racking experience. There is no way of dropping a ship out of sight and it makes for a very big target. But, as Healey, one of the 258 pilots left behind in Singapore because he had no machine to fly and who was attacked when escaping on the *Empire Star*, most graphically recounted to me, a cool commander soon got the hang of how to minimize the risk. What he had to do was watch through binoculars for the opening of the aircraft bomb doors and at once take evasive action; the course adopted by the enemy bombers and the rigid timing of the delivery of the bombs after the bays had opened almost invariably ensured that the target would be missed. Healey's ship came through, damaged it is true, after several hours of almost incessant bombing, but Doorman's fleet was quite unscathed. What is difficult to understand is why it was that Doorman, if it had been considered worthwhile setting out to attack a more powerful fleet in the first place, having survived without loss or damage bombing attacks lasting for several hours, should have decided to withdraw. One suspects that Doorman himself would subsequently have found it difficult to answer this question – he is quoted as saying that history would condemn him for the retirement. But retire he did. With only four hours of daylight left during which he would remain at risk from aircraft attack, and when sufficiently close to the invasion fleet to have been able to intercept it before dawn of 16 February, he ordered withdrawal back to Java via the Gaspar Strait. The last chance of seriously impeding the invasion of Sumatra had been lost.

11
The Final Resistance

The records covering the operations on 15 February as compiled by Lyster for the official RAAF history are no longer confined to the efforts of the two Australian squadrons but cover both the British echelons and, to a degree, operations by 232 and 258 Squadrons:

"As a result of an electrical storm on the night of 14 February the telephone line from P.2 to 225 Group H.Q. in Palembang was disrupted; and as this had been the only means of communication, the station was left to its own resources.

"The night of 14 February was given over to preparations for first light attack on the enemy forces approaching from the sea. Our forces consisted of 38 Blenheims and Hudsons, together with 22 Hurricanes but of these only 35 were operationally serviceable by first light of the fifteenth. At dawn of 15 February reconnaissance aircraft pinpointed the position of enemy transports and landing barges. Approximately 20 warships and barges and transports were steaming through the Banka Straits, while other transports and landing craft were swarming round the estuaries of the Moesi and adjacent rivers.

"All reconnaissance, except an hourly one of the roads and rivers radiating from Palembang, was discontinued and full-scale bombing and strafing operations were commenced against the invasion forces.

"The first sortie was planned for three Hudsons and three Blenheims to be escorted by some Hurricanes but a heavy fog caused an alteration. At 0630 hours three Hudsons, one from No. 1 Squadron and the other two from No. 8 Squadron, took off slightly in advance of the three Blenheims. The Hurricane escort took off but they tried to remain below the fog and, finding it too dangerous, returned to land.

"The Hudsons proceeded unescorted above the fog. Over Palembang this force met an enemy fighter screen so they entered the fog to escape detection. They flew north and when they came again out of the fog they encountered Navy '0's which attacked them. The No. 1 Squadron Hudson now became separated from its fellows and after three further attempts to come out of the fog, each time encountering fighters, it returned to P.2 under cover of the fog. The other two aircraft succeeded in evading the enemy and the captains, Flt. Lt. R. Widmer and Flg. Off. Lower, sighted twenty-three warships and merchant vessels in the Banka Strait. They proceeded to attack a small vessel which was escorted by two destroyers and scored near misses.

"The three Blenheims similarly met some twenty-six Navy '0's while over P.1. One Blenheim got through immediately and proceeded over the target, scoring several near misses on a 4,000 ton vessel. The other two Blenheims, after three attempts to shake off the fighter screen, attacked the landing forces and sank five or six troop-carrying barges. All six aircraft of this sortie returned individually to P.2. Both in the fog and out of it the visibility had been very poor, due to the burning oil tanks to the N.E. of Palembang.

"The second striking force, consisting of three Hudsons of 62 Squadron, met no enemy aircraft. They bombed at low level and scored a direct hit on a 5,000-ton merchant vessel, though heavy fire from cruisers prevented them from seeing the result of the hit. On approaching Palembang the three Hudsons machine-gunned barges on the river. They met with enemy fighters over P.1 and one of our rear gunners shot one of them down.

"The third striking force consisted of nine Blenheims. They attacked a 4,000-ton merchant vessel in formation and scored direct hits. The vessel was later confirmed as having been sunk as the same pilots on a later sortie saw survivors being picked up on the spot where the attack had been made.

"The fourth striking force consisted of six Blenheims and ten Hurricanes. The Blenheims attacked a 3,500-ton vessel at low level and direct hits set her on fire. The Hurricanes after providing cover for the striking force, carried out individual attacks on troop-carrying barges on the rivers and returned to P.2.

"Two RAF pilots who were without aircraft asked permission to take up the two non-operational Blenheims of 27 Squadron. This was refused them, so they themselves worked for three hours on the aircraft and brought them to a serviceable condition, and were then given permission to take them up. These two Blenheims then proceeded to carry out individual strafing runs on enemy barges. Such are the pleasureable exertions of victory.

"The fifth striking force consisted of six Blenheims. They attacked ships which had been lying off Banka Island and which had just proceeded to sea past the mouth of the Palembang River. These ships were escorted by two destroyers. One direct hit was scored on the bow of a merchant vessel of 8,000–10,000 tons which caught fire and developed a heavy list. The Blenheims then strafed troops on the side of this ship at deck level, using the side guns until all ammunition was exhausted.

"The sixth and final sortie was carried out at 1405 hours by two Mk III Hudsons of No. 8 Squadron escorted by eight Hurricanes. The captains of these Hudson aircraft were Flg. Off. Stumm and Flg. Off. Richards (RAF).

"It will be as well to insert at this point some explanation for the appearance of RAF officers' names in No. 8 Squadron diary. The pilots who had ferried out the Mk III Hudsons from the Middle East were kept on in Sumatra and were glad of any opportunity to fly.

"The Hudsons attacked destroyers and merchant vessels and scored a direct hit on an 8,000-ton ship, and two very near misses on a 6,000-ton ship. Both Hudsons and Hurricanes then strafed the decks of the two destroyers from mast height. Enemy fighters with fixed undercarriages attempted to interfere and two of them were shot down by the Hurricanes. Flg. Off. Richard's second pilot, who was also acting as a gunner, Sqn. Ldr. Garrard, was also credited with having shot down an enemy fighter. Their Hudson was badly holed with incendiary bullets and Sqn. Ldr. Garrard was wounded but the aircraft managed to return to P2.

"Throughout the day, when not providing escort cover, the Hurricanes continuously landed, re-armed and refuelled and returned to strafing attacks against troop carrying barges.

"The last operation of the Hurricanes was against a large number of aircraft that were sighted on a beach on the S.W. of Banka Island. These aircraft were the Navy '0's that had earlier provided the fighter screen for the enemy landing. Their carrier had been sunk, presumably by a Dutch submarine, and as their fuel had given out they had been forced to land on the beach. There they provided an easy target."

There follows a summary of the results claimed concluding: 'The number of Japanese killed cannot be estimated. The pilots could only give fanciful comparisons, as for example, comparing Moesi River to a bowl of water in which a box of matches could have been emptied, and a horrifying sense of the banks being littered with bodies. The Flight Commanders of the Hurricanes, who were very experienced pilots, gave it as their opinion, that they had never seen such heavy damage inflicted.'

I have to say that I find the report of strafing the Japanese aircraft which had landed on a beach somewhat bewildering. Apart from the fact that one would be fortunate indeed to force-land one fighter aircraft on a sand beach successfully, let alone an aircraft carrier's complement, I have never heard this story from anywhere else and after all knew personally most of the Hurricane pilots involved. Neither have I discovered any record nor heard from any other source that the aircraft-carrier *Ryuku* was sunk off Banka. On the other hand there are photographic records of carrier *Ryukaku* (surely the same ship) being attacked by American aircraft later on that year.

Like all reports of air warfare, Mr Lyster's has to be taken with a considerable degree of caution. Although of course slow in comparison with modern machines, the aircraft used, Blenheims, Hudsons and Hurricanes, still moved very swiftly, and when attacks are made at low level the target is soon left behind. Moreover whilst in action, especially when every ship in sight is hurling everything it can at the attacking aircraft or enemy fighters are about their business, the adrenalin is flowing very fast indeed and one's heart is at a gallop – it needs

a very special type of young man to observe results dispassion-
ately and the temptation to indulge in a little wishful thinking is
difficult to resist. The victories claimed in the Battle of Britain
far exceeded the number of aircraft which the records showed
to have been lost to the Luftwaffe in that remarkable summer.
To state this truism, or for that matter to comment specifically
on the accuracy of any part of Mr Lyster's record, is in no way
to denigrate the efforts or dedication of the Blenheim and
Hudson pilots involved. As one of the Hurricane pilots who was
on P.2 at the time, I am only too conscious of how little
protection we fighter pilots gave to the bombers involved.

Mr Lyster's report errs where it describes the problems of the
Hurricane escort to the first sortie and, I feel sure, the number
of serviceable Hurricanes at P.2 at the time. I was one of the
pilots who took part in that first flight early on the morning of
the 15th. Eight of us took off. We did not try to remain below the
fog – it would have been a practical impossibility to remain
below the 'fog' for it was, in fact, a very thin layer of mist whose
base was barely above tree-top level. From the ground this
layer appeared so thin as to present no obvious problems and
the sun could be seen through it quite clearly; from above it
blanketed off the whole of Sumatra, or at least as far as the eye
could see in every direction. To crews of Blenheims or Hudsons
it had nuisance value only, for they had the range to seek
alternative airfields if necessary; to Hurricane pilots it presented insuperable problems. Once through the layer all that
could be seen was a sheet of smooth white cloud stretching to
the horizon while the airfield, the only one to which we had the
range to return, had disappeared. It was somewhere there
below and a little behind us. We had no means of ever finding it
again for there were no sophisticated systems, such as radio
direction-finding, in being in Sumatra such as were available to
fighter pilots in the UK. Indeed had it not been for the quick
thinking of one of our American pilots there is no doubt almost
the last few Hurricanes available in Sumatra would have been
lost in a single mission. Donahue, who was leading the strike
force, appreciated the danger the moment he entered the mist,
immediately banged down his undercarriage lever and,
because of P.2's enormous size, was able to land safely on his
take-off run. Hurriedly finding a Very pistol, he raced to the

middle of the field firing cartridges through the mist which, exploding like roman candles above it, gave the unhappy pilots now mislaid in a void a point around which to circle while trying to decide what they should do next. As both Donahue in his *Last Flight from Singapore* and I in my *Hurricane Over the Jungle* have described the nerve-racking ordeal (as seen both from above and below) of somehow getting down again on to an airfield bordered by trees whose tops are in cloud, I will not repeat it here. I will, however, take the opportunity of making one correction to the account in my book: Donahue was not, as I have stated, the sole pilot with sufficient presence of mind to realize that once through that innocuous-looking skein of mist it might be impossible to do more than fly around vaguely hoping it would clear and then if it hadn't by the time fuel was exhausted bale out into jungle, swamp, or sea. Lambert also, as he has since informed me, shoved the nose and undercarriage down in time and landed safely.

All eight of us managed to put down again on P.2 but one Hurricane ended up on its nose and one on its back. This, incidentally, is no reflection on the pilots' skill – landing on P.2 was always a risky sort of business. Apart from odd trees which grew in the middle of the field and deep ruts left by taxiing aircraft, the ground was in parts very soft and the aircraft's wheels simply dug into it and stuck. At least one of the two Hurricanes put out of commission was seen by Lambert to suffer this fate: "Having brought my aircraft to a standstill, I saw another Hurricane coming in to land on a similar path to myself and about to pass me before coming to rest, and still with a fair burst of speed on, when the undercarriage simply went into a lot of soft muddy ground we had all experienced before and went straight over on its back. That pilot, I think, was named Fleming. I immediately left my aircraft and by that time Donahue and one or two more on the ground had managed to get a truck out to Fleming's aircraft and we lifted one of the main planes up and wedged the truck underneath it in order to release a somewhat shaken but, I believe, not badly injured Fleming."

So far as I was personally concerned after several hair-raising attempts to get down had failed, I solved the problem by using P.2's enormous size to carry out a steep turn (with wheels and flaps both down) at one end of it at a height of something less than fifty feet and luckily got away with it.

Anyway we still had six usable machines and, possibly, more. According to my own notes, 232 Squadron made a strafing attack on the self-propelled barges packed with Japanese now making their slow way up the Moesi. The 232 Squadron records make no mention of this, but these records were, of course, compiled some weeks later only from memory and the facts as known to the writer at the time while the pilots who would have been involved were by then either dead, or prisoners or (in the case of eight of them) in Australia. At all events whether or not 232 made such an attack, 258 Squadron did so at least once, possibly twice, later in the morning. I was one of the pilots involved flying operationally twice more that day. My recollections of one flight are quite hazy; I think it must have either been an abortive flight or the targets found were only minor craft. The other flight I remember very well. I flew Number Two to Donahue, another of our five American pilots. As again our experiences are fully recorded in both *Last Flight from Singapore* and *Hurricane Over the Jungle*, I will only recount them briefly.

The oil wells had now been fired and a great column of intense black smoke rose high into the sky to level off and drift in a very broad swathe in, as I recall, a north-easterly direction. Under cover of this shield for at least part of the way, we set off for the Moesi. I do not know how many of the others found the barges but at least Donahue and I, split off from the rest, did so. I flew behind Donahue as he made his first attack which he executed brilliantly. The barges at the point where we came upon them were, unluckily for their occupants, on a straight piece of the river so that they were in line astern. They were packed with infantry like sardines in a tin and their sole defence was a machine-gun mounted at the back. A Hurricane with twelve guns had a fire-power of about twelve thousand rounds a minute, with eight guns, eight thousand. I don't know which we were flying — we had some of both. I watched the bullets from Donahue's guns forming a pincushion behind the rear-most barge, moving along both sides of it, and then poppling the water between it and the barge ahead. And so along the

Flying Officer 'Art' Donahue DFC, another of the American pilots.

line. The casualties he caused must have been ferocious. I could see both the flicker of the defenders' machine-guns and the path and flash of the tracer bullets which formed part of the arming of our machine-guns for combat.

Donahue made only the single run having been (unknown by me) hit by a machine-gun bullet. Somewhat mystified by his departure, I made three attacks before returning to P.2 where I learnt he had been wounded and already taken away for treatment. He was invalided to UK and, making a complete recovery, was given command of a Spitfire squadron in England. Sadly he was to lose his life in operations over the Channel that same autumn.

There is no doubt that the casualties we inflicted on the Advance Force were horrendous and when, as prisoners of war we discovered that the effect of Hurricane strafing were spoken of by the Japanese with awe, we hastily removed the brevets from our shirts. Nevertheless by early afternoon the last operational flight had been made by 258 Squadron in Sumatra. This fact has always baffled me. The barges were still making their way up the Moesi (and, although we did not know this at the time, the Salang and Telang Rivers) and we still had Hurricanes, and presumably ammunition. On the sorties completed we had inflicted horrendous casualties and lost no Hurricanes in the process. Yet we were ordered to evacuate to Java. I think the answer has to be that the sense of panic generally prevailing clouded calm and reasoned judgement for there was still not one Japanese soldier within forty or fifty miles. I wrote: 'We sat around watching, rather gloomily, an impressive oil fire somewhere near at hand. There was a terrible atmosphere of depression and defeat; much the same as in Singapore and yet in a way more tangible. One almost expected Japanese suddenly to rush us from the jungle. We ate tinned sausages and wondered what was going to happen next – we hadn't any Hurricanes. Others had taken them. I don't know who. Then came the casual, weary order that we were on our own. We walked down the lane which led to the airfield. A rutted sort of track with low thick bushes on either hand. We knew quite well that there weren't any enemy in miles but we still felt uneasy. The track came to a T-junction. To the left it led to the railway station and the road to Palembang, to the right to the airfield. We held a council of war – which way to go?'

Thus are decisions made which change men's lives. Two of us decided to try our luck on the airfield; the others to try the railway. Those who tried the railway ended up by escaping to Ceylon and freedom; we did not for we both found Hurricanes. For my part I found the very aircraft I had done most of my flying in in Sumatra. It was defined unserviceable so, presumably, another pilot, perhaps of 232, may have made a further strafing run. I can't remember what was the matter with it; I do remember the ground staff warned me not to fly it, that I chose to do so rather than be left alone the only 258 pilot, amongst all that gloom and misery, that it veered madly to port on take-off and I all but hit a hut. However it got me safely down to Java.

There is a curious sequel to this story. Some forty years after this incident, I was telephoned by Ted Read, who had been in the same prison camps with me in Java and Japan, who told me of a painting at an aeronautical artists' exhibition in Derby which would, he thought, interest me. My wife and I went to have a look, liked the painting and bought it. It was a painting by Miles O'Reilly of a Hurricane just taking off from a jungle airfield and its title was intriguing: *Departure from P.2*. When the painting was delivered I found O'Reilly's telephone number on the back. I contacted him. How on earth, I asked, had he come to paint such a picture? Even to know of P.2? The answer was simple: he had read *Hurricane Over the Jungle* and my account of the last Hurricane to leave Sumatra being taken off had inspired him! Well I was now rather proud of that painting so I had him come round and touch it up: putting the correct squadron letters and even the number of the machine – 5481 – on it. The squadron letters were a bit of a cheat for we never had time to paint them on our Hurricanes and flew them bland and naked. Still it seemed the right thing to have him do. The painting hangs in my dining-room and is a useful prop if conversation languishes. It has also been reproduced and forms the jacket cover to this book.

For RAF fighter pilots the war was, on the whole, a gentlemanly affair. Not for them the dust of parade grounds, the mud of trenches, the exposure to Atlantic blizzards. Under normal circumstances they were collected from their billets by truck and delivered to their dispersal points where, when not flying, they sat around top buttons undone, illegal silk scarves tucked into their necks, playing poker, reading *Picture Post* or snoozing the day away. And even in the hurly-burly and confusion of the Far East war, this system in a rough-and-ready way applied.

Not so their ground staffs. Their lot was far less organized and far more uncomfortable. And certainly not for them was escape from doomed Sumatra by swift, clean flight a possibility. In saying this I do not overlook the other Allied troops in Palembang – but these were very few: the ack-ack gunners and a small number of Army and Navy personnel who, almost accidentally, found themselves in a war zone where they had no apparent role or purpose.

For these men the balloon had well and truly, as they say, gone up. Panic stalked the streets of Palembang, there were paratroops under every bed and hordes of Japanese were swarming up the rivers. Rumour was extinguished only by counter-rumour. Flight was the order of the day. Before there had been little by way of organization; now there was none at all. The Dutch, theoretically, were in command. But the Dutch had no plan and no cohesion and the RAF men they came upon wandering bewilderedly around the town in their inappropriate khaki uniforms were curious specimens for whom they had neither time nor respect nor interest. They were, on the whole, abandoned to their own devices.

The picture, surely, can be no better painted than by these men themselves.

Had Thomas Macaulay lived in a later age and been in Palembang at the time, he might well have used Corporal A. ('Soapy') Hudson as his model rather than Horatius, for, excepting only that Hudson had just one, rather than two, companions, to guard his bridge, there was a remarkable similarity between them.

'Soapy' Hudson. Photograph taken before embarkation to Far East.

Hudson, together with his friend Leading Aircraftman Ted Parsons, found themselves near a group of young children and their teachers (who were nuns) and were ordered by an army officer to escort these refugees to a train. When they had done so a second army officer, who happened to be by the siding, then ordered Hudson and Parsons (who between them possessed a Lewis gun and one pan of ammunition and two rifles and about twenty rounds which they had picked up off the street in Palembang) to stand guard at a nearby concrete bridge over the river so as to be able to warn the train driver if the Japanese came in sight. After another half-hour or so, an army staff car drove up and a third officer ordered them to hold the bridge until all his guns had passed over. This was all a bit above their heads, but they nodded dumbly and the officer, as if this were part of a seriously worked-out plan, turned his car and drove back down the road. No guns appeared but about fifteen minutes later an RAF sergeant, driving an army truck, came up to the bridge, enquired what they were doing and on being told responded laconically that they were 'nuts' and continued on his way. A suspicious silence now fell which was finally broken by the sound of a motor boat put-putting up the river and taking a look at this, Hudson and Parsons discovered it was full of Japanese. Unenthusiastically, they discussed the possibility of doing something about the matter only to come to the conclusion that the range was too great for them to do anything but draw attention to themselves. The Japanese then drove their boat to the opposite bank, climbed ashore and disappeared from view.

By now Hudson and Parsons felt very much indeed like Horatius, Lartius and Herminius, sole guardians of a bridge not against Lars Porsena and his Tuscan hordes but against Tanaka and his swarming Japanese. To use Hudson's own words: 'It began to dawn on us that we could very shortly be in some trouble.' However, at that moment, they were amazed to see a Dutch army officer appear, as it were from nowhere, climbing up on to the middle of the bridge. He looked at them in some surprise and then remarked: 'I think you had better go along to the train. I am about to blow this bridge up.' So they went along to the train only to be approached by yet another officer, this time of the Royal Navy, whose eyes lit up when he saw their armaments. 'Ah! Just what I want!' he cried, pointing to the Lewis gun.

So 'Soapy' and Ted ended up behind the engine with a new assignment – to repel any Japanese who attempted to come aboard. There was a bit of a hitch before they pulled out in that the driver, in fact giving them 'more trouble than the Japs' was refusing to drive the train but the naval officer solved this small difficulty by pulling out a revolver and holding it to the poor fellow's head and after that they had no further trouble and were driven at speed to Oosthaven.

Hedley Bonnes recounts – "We were the wrong side of the Moesi and we had no transport at all at that time and I remember seeing an Australian officer in this empty hotel . . . everything was empty at that time. There were one or two Dutch soldiers about and we had no maps and this Australian officer, who was wounded by the way, couldn't get around very much, he was going to stay there and he gave us a piece of map. Obviously torn out of a book or something like that. We went down to the river and scrounged around a bit and we found a launch, an RAF launch, tied up there. I can't remember if it had the roundels on it or not but it was an air sea rescue thing they were using. So we – there were about twelve of us by this time – we belted across the river in rather a hurry and the other side of the river we parked this thing and we got out of it and searched around for some other means of transport. The only thing we could find was a native bloke fooling round with an old lorry in a sort of garage, shed sort of thing. And we persuaded him to let us have this lorry. Mind you we were armed and he wasn't and he hadn't much chance, poor chap. So we swapped this launch, rather expensive launch, for this old lorry, you see. Always remember the name of the lorry – it was 'Globe' and I've never heard of a Globe. We put some drums of petrol on board and away we went. We went tootling down.

"Now I can't remember where we went, I wasn't navigating or doing anything like that at all, I was standing on the back of the lorry. From somewhere I'd liberated a tommy gun, I don't know what the hell we were going to do with it because they're useless things anyway. And we went on down and we finished up in some damn back track place, the devil if I know where we were. And at one point we got so lost that we had to go across a bamboo bridge. Now when I say a bamboo bridge, it was a sort of swing bridge thing and to get a lorry across that was not funny. So we all got off the lorry and the driver volunteered – well there was no one else who could drive it anyway, he had to take this thing across. Which he did. And what happened then? That's right. After a number of hours – we were rather hungry at the time – we came to a *kampong*, you know the usual *kampong* thing, and we parked ourselves there and we got some food, coconuts, bananas and all that sort of nonsense and stayed the night there.

"We left early the next morning because we were told the Japanese were fairly close. Afterwards I heard the story, now I don't know whether this referred to the *kampong* we were in, the locals we were with, but it was certainly true of some other characters. They were put in the long house or whatever it was they called it in this *kampong*. In the morning there was a hell of a hue and cry going on because they'd been looking out for some toilet paper – they found an old book in this place which they promptly used for toilet paper, you see. It happened to be the Koran! So they fobbed them off by giving them about four hundred Malay dollars and a copy of *KRRs*. [King's Regulations] Now I can't swear to the *KRRs* – I think it was a bit of an exaggeration . . . I don't think we'd run round Sumatra with the Japanese after us with a copy of *KRRs*!

"Anyway from there we tootled on and after a bit we found this lorry was not very well, in fact the damn thing was boiling over like blazes all the time which was rather unfortunate because we didn't want to waste the water we had in our water bottles so we did, honestly, use the obvious method of filling the radiator with water, you know. It was great, it worked you know, but if you've ever driven, sitting on the top of a lorry with it blowing off steam from a mixture of airmen's pee and it's wafting all over you . . . You've never smelt anything like it in your life, you know. No wonder the Japanese never caught up with us! They wouldn't get near us!

"Anyway we breezed on for a time and we got to P.2. When we got there everything was blasted well burnt. Huts filled with tinned food and all burnt. And we had no food at all. They'd wrecked everything. And we found out later the Japs were never anywhere near P.2. They didn't even know that it existed! Well this Globe lorry was just about conking out and I had a scrounge down the road and there was a jolly good lorry in a ditch, you could see it could be moved out and I was fooling around with that thing trying to move it, trying to get the engine started and a blessed Dutch officer came along in a rather posh uniform, and in one of these wooden holster things, a Luger. He was going to shoot me! For deserting! He spoke reasonable English. Well good enough English for me to know what he was talking about! And I said don't do that, I'm just trying to shift the lorry on to P.2. He told me to buzz off and leave the lorry alone, which I did. And we carried on, in this clapped out Globe and we came to a railway line and knew we were somewhere near to civilization. So we abandoned the lorry, which was by this time *absolutely* clapped out, and there were people around trying to get on this train. And finally, hell of a long time afterwards, must have been about next morning I think, a train came through pulling a whole load of flat cars full of refugees and one thing and another. But we were able to get on and we carried on down and got to Oosthaven."

Tom Jackson describes this train in the diary he wrote at the time: "P.2 was just disorganised shambles. Everybody was milling around getting nowhere; no one knew a damn thing. I eventually climbed aboard a lorry which was full of Aussies and we set off in the direction of Oosthaven. There were twenty or thirty of us in the lorry and it wasn't particularly big either. In the early afternoon we arrived at some place or other at which we stopped and had a bite to eat, mainly bananas and fruit. We were just waiting to start again when we heard a train whistle in the distance. The officer in charge of the lorry said we would be better off travelling by train so we beetled off to the station and a large amount of flannelling saw us ensconced in a first class carriage in a siding. Then the train came along. What a sight it was! There were no carriages – just trucks and open wagons. It looked as though every truck had been covered with glue and half the world's population thrown on it. Men were hanging on to the buffers, perched on the engine, sitting on the edges – they were everywhere. Natives and whites mixed. Dutch troops, RAF personnel, sailors, soldiers, women and children, Indians and Chinamen. Rags and tatters seemed to be the most popular dress, stubble trouble was prevalent and all the white people were black from the charcoal burning engine. I reckoned I was darned lucky to have a seat in a coach. What a difference there was between this luxury compartment and the coaches we'd travelled *up* to Palembang in. This one had plush seats, green coloured sun-shade glass in the windows, good ventilation, a bar (empty), and tables. We reached Oosthaven late at night and slept on crates of bully beef and camp pie."

A number of 258 Squadron pilots were fortunate enough to have a Hurricane in which to fly down to Batavia. But on the whole the squadron was badly scattered. Of its original complement of twenty-four pilots, five – McAlister, Glynn, Keedwell, Kleckner and (Pilot Officer) Scott – were dead; four – Donahue, Campbell-White, Nash and Nichols – were injured; Geffene (the fifth American) had been mislaid *en route*, forced-landing in Algeciras, Spain (from whence he escaped rejoining the reformed squadron in Ceylon and being shot down and killed in the Japanese Easter Day raid on Trincomalee). Healey had been left behind in Singapore; Sharp was missing; and Milnes, McCulloch, (Sergeant) Scott, Cicurel, Campbell and Macnamara had last been seen in Palembang while our sole Australian pilot, Sheerin, was, I believe, one of those who decided to try for the road and railway rather than look for a Hurricane on the field and he too escaped to Ceylon. It would seem probable that the other five (Thomson, de la Perelle, Dobbyn, Lambert and myself) all flew from P.2 to Kemajoran Airport, Batavia.

Milnes and Nichols managed by joining up with some 232 Squadron pilots in the town and commandeering a car which they drove south until they reached a railway station and, exchanging the car for tickets, got comfortably down to Oosthaven. Scott made his own way to the port, probably by train, and, I believe joining Sheerin, boarded a ship whose captain refused to allow them to land when it called in at Java and thus he too escaped to Colombo. The others had more unusual journeys.

Pilot Officers 'Micky' Nash (showing throat
wound inflicted by paratroops), Ambrose Milnes
and Campbell White.

Sergeant Pilot Ken
('Junior') Glynn, the
youngest of the sergeant
pilots.

Campbell writes of his own: "We got back to town and McCulloch showed up at this time. He'd got quite a story. Seems he'd been shot down and when he landed it was actually beside another Hurricane that was on its back beside a river bank and I believe that was Glynn's crash. He couldn't do anything for Junior who was dead, but there were these natives and he tried to get them to give him a hand but they just stayed sort of off at a distance, so he inflated his dinghy and got in the river. And these natives were just standing at a distance so he took his pistol and fired a couple of shots over their heads and they ran off. And when I asked him why he'd done that, he said: 'Well if the buggers weren't going to help me, I certainly didn't want them standing there and staring at me.' So then he paddled his way down river till he hit a fork which allowed him to come back up river to Palembang. And there he was. And we had Tudor (Tudor Jones, 258 Squadron Engineering Officer) and this enlisted L.A.C. Peter something, I can't ever remember his last name, had found a Dutch river patrol boat. It had two small Ford V.8. engines in it and it had a mounting for a machine gun on it. And so we decided to commandeer this thing. The problem with it was, one of the propellers was badly bent. It had apparently run aground somewhere – I guess why it had been left. But we decided to take this and go – we looked at a map and decided we could go up river and intersect the road for P.2 and rejoin our people. We arrived there late in the evening and there were people coming down the road heading in the other direction who led us to understand the Japanese were just over the next hill which we found out later was complete cock but at the time we believed them. So we decided then that our only recourse was to stay with the boat and get as far south as we could and get away from the immediate area. So that's what we did. We spent the rest of that day and we called in at night and then the next day on the boat – gosh, I can't recall just how many days we did spend. But anyway we finally were starting to run out of river bottom . . . we kept running aground. We came to a native village and Ting Macnamara exercised his usual charm and between him and Cicurel, they talked the local natives by sign language and so forth into trading a lorry they had there for this lovely boat which they thought was really great. I don't think they owned the lorry

Moesi River escapers in southern Sumatran village.
Left to right: Tudor Jones, Campbell, Cicurel,
Lamont and Macnamara.

either.

"Anyway we took the lorry and all our gear – we had taken all the arms we could carry in the boat. We drove the lorry and we finally came to a bridge that had been blown. This was after . . . I don't know how many miles . . . and by this time it was evening. We got across the river and walked all that night. I couldn't do it today if I had to. Also I wouldn't be as frightened today, I guess. But I carried a rifle, a Tommy gun and two pistols and a knapsack with a lot of my personal gear in it. I don't know how many miles we walked that night. It must have been at least fifteen . . . some place between fifteen and twenty miles we walked that night and the next day, and finally came on an intersection in the road where there were people coming down another road and we got a ride down into the south end of Sumatra – probably the last twenty-five miles – where we got passage on a ferry that was going over to Java and that's the way we made our way back to Batavia."

We can return to the New Zealander, Denny Sharp, who, it will be recalled, had arrived at Bencoolen on the west coast and was being requested by the owner of a Chevrolet to drive him and some other Dutchmen to a conference at a small village some miles inland. "So, [he reports], I drove these Dutch people out to this village for their conference. I can't remember how many Dutch people there were but there must have been four, five or six. So we drove out to this village and we had the conference in the village hall or school. It was quite interesting because they were talking in Dutch all the time and then when they made their decision they would communicate it to me in English. And they had decided that they were going to form a guerilla band and go into the hills and fight the Japanese from the hills. They asked me to join them. No way was I going to join them. So I told them this and they said: 'Okay, we'll leave things as they are. We're going up into the jungle, you're not coming and we're going back to the hotel to spend the night and decide exactly what's going to happen.' So back to the hotel we go and once again I put through a call to this Wing Commander and he said: 'Yes, the boat was coming in but he couldn't give the exact time.' On the morning of the sixteenth then, I rang the Wing Commander again and the boat had still not arrived so I told him that we had made plans meantime and that we were going to drive down the coast as far south as possible, as far south as the vehicle would get, and pick up a native boat, or boats and that we were going to row down the coast and across the Sunda Strait even if we had to paddle. And that was my intention. He says well okay you do that. Now by this time about twenty or thirty airmen had arrived in Bencoolen and they were sitting around with no leader to tell them what to do and I told them the situation about the boat coming down and it may arrive here, it may not arrive here. And I told them that my decision was to go south as far as possible along the coast and, if I had to, get a boat of some description and sail south, cross the Sunda Strait and into Java.

"I don't think there were many good sailors amongst them because not many of them decided to come with us but we set off along the coast road to a place called Bentuan (now Bintuhan) which was about another fifty miles south of Bencoolen. It was a small jungle road one car wide; if you met some passing traffic you'd have had to draw off into the verge at the side. But we didn't meet any passing traffic, fortunately, and we had quite an uneventful drive to this place called Bentuan. We had one interesting experience when we had to ferry this car, this Chev, which the Dutchman had given me, across a river, not very wide, but swift flowing. It was only about forty yards wide and it was on a bamboo raft and it was difficult to manoeuvre the thing. I thought the thing was going to capsize. But nevertheless we sent somebody across and they freed the raft from the other side, pulled it across with bamboo raffia jungle cord. We manhandled the car on to the bamboo raft and pulled it across to the other side and everything went well, it took a long time, but eventually we got across and set further south on our journey.

"We arrived at this place called Bentuan round about four o'clock in the afternoon and I rang the Wing Commander again and he could still not give me any information about this boat. So I said I'd ring him in the morning and that if he didn't have any good news we were going to head off into the jungle. We slept in a school and we met up with another twenty or thirty airmen who'd got there somehow and were also waiting for transport to get them down to Java. The next day, the seventeenth I think it was, we made ready a couple of lighters in case this boat came down and we were also going to use them if we had to go down the coast and I rang up and somebody told me that the boat had arrived, they'd all gone aboard and they were going to call in at Bentuan and pick us up. So we made ready these lighters for the dual purpose either of getting out to this boat or sailing down the coast and eventually the boat arrived round about midday. We loaded everybody on this tramp steamer – it wasn't very big, it was only about three or four thousand tons – and the last thing I did, which broke my heart, I drove this nice Chevrolet, it wasn't very old, couldn't have been more than about six months old, I drove it straight into the surf. It was a pleasure on the one hand to do a thing like this but on the other hand to wreck a car like that, it broke my heart. Nevertheless we got aboard this boat and we were pretty tired so it didn't take much to get to sleep and next day we'd crossed the Sunda Strait and arrived at Batavia. And it was there that I rejoined part of 258 Squadron."

12
Escape from Sumatra

Although evacuation of P.2 had commenced during the morning of 15 February, the airfield, as has been seen, continued to be used for operational purposes for a good portion of the day. Apart from the attacks upon the convoy in the Banka Strait and Tanaka's troops advancing up the Moesi, Hudsons were flown up through the day from Java for the purpose of collecting Squadron Commanders and other important personnel. The great majority of ground personnel were however shifted out in an orderly enough fashion, the system being to drive them in groups to Parambuli some twenty-five or so miles south of P.2 where they were unloaded and instructed to walk the rest of the way to the railhead while the transport returned to collect further groups. By this means some twelve hundred men were evacuated with the final twenty led by the Station Commander, the Australian Group Captain McCauley, just after 6 p.m. The only men left behind were a small party under the command of the Station Armament Officer to supplement the Dutch Army garrison and 'complete the denial plan' and another small group who had the lonely task of making airworthy three unserviceable Blenheims. These Blenheims successfully reached Java but a fourth, which from a cursory inspection appeared airworthy, having been taken off with a fair number of passengers crammed into it, soon demonstrated the reason for its abandonment when one of its wings evinced signs of stress. When this wing was actually seen to be moving, the pilot decided to crash-land and following a river finally came to a place where it broadened to a lake. Not daring to circle he was obliged hastily to take the one chance of belly-flopping offered but failed to carry this out successfully with the result that the aircraft broke in two and all aboard were killed except for one very lucky man, in the well of the plane, a storekeeper named Shaw, who, recovering conscious-ness under the surface, struggled up and, looking about him, saw a petrol tank which had broken free bobbing nearby. Although badly injured he was able to utilize this offering (a most fortuitous one as he couldn't swim) to keep afloat until some natives rowed out in canoes and towed him to the bank, from whence he made his way to Java and, eventually, a prison camp.

An extraordinary story, but I have had it from several sources including Bob Chapman of 605 Squadron and Eric Rice who was a Flight Sergeant in charge of Maintenance Flight of 84 Squadron both of whom have provided me with much useful information.

For ships between the mouth of the Moesi and Palembang itself there was now, of course, no possibility of escape. Cooper commanding the *Jerantut* and Smythe commanding the *Klias*, both of which had arrived at the port by dawn of the 15th, had been ordered to sink their ships to block the river near the coal wharf and the railway station. Cordite was laid around *Klias'* decks and a box of fireworks placed on the galley stove to act as a fuse in the hope that after the sea-cocks had been opened and the vessel had partially sunk the subsequent explosion would render the possibility of subsequent salvage and removal more difficult. Unfortunately, much to Smythe's fury, *Klias* settled on her side and the hoped-for explosion failed to take place.

Cooper and Smythe, together with Brown of the *Hua Tong*, remained with a party to destroy river craft and then set about extricating themselves and a party of about one hundred leaderless men of the Army Pay Corps and the like (who had presented themselves) from the clutches of the Japanese. They found the town in a state of chaos and investigating a small railway terminus found that all the engines had been sabotaged. However one engine appeared chugging up the line to collect a Dutch official with much baggage and overtake the last train. Smythe boarded this engine (which was being driven by an Eurasian driver) with a small but heavily armed party to bring it back to Palembang to make up a train while Cooper started sending the troops down the line. While accompanying them he was stopped by a Eurasian bearing a document. Cooper had left the *Jerantut* still equipped with his 'golf shoes and navy raincoat with bully beef and odd cigarettes' in his pocket and still wore a tin hat. The Eurasian enquired if he was an officer to which an answer was given in no uncertain terms by a stoker of some six feet four inches height who had originally been on the *Prince of Wales* and latterly had formed part of the *Jerantut* crew. The Eurasian, reassured, offered his document (which required an authorization to blow up an oil park of some twenty tanks) to Cooper who, naturally enough, hesitated. However the stoker suggested that if he signed it 'Lieutenant Fred Karno' there could hardly be a come-back later. Cooper duly did so and the Eurasian 'went off happily, used his plunger and the oil park went up'.

Meanwhile Smythe turned up with the railway engine and together they went along the railway line picking up troops as and when they caught up with them passing *en route* between the blazing oil tanks for whose destruction Cooper had given authority and in due course, after one or two hiccups, their numbers hugely increased, they reached Oosthaven. Smythe was in due course to escape to Colombo while Cooper, after taking to the jungle in Java and eluding the Japanese for several months, was finally betrayed and sent to the native gaol of Boei Glodok in Batavia where I, and all the 258 Squadron pilots who had survived but failed to get away, were also prisoners. He was later to travel with me on the notorious *Dai Nichi Maru* and then to the same camp near Hiroshima.

So far as the other individuals who had escaped from Singapore and whose fortunes we have been following are concerned, Brigadier Bird, it will be recalled, had been left with two other men sitting on a Carley float in the middle of the South China Sea while Major Donald Wright and his party had reached a small village some thirty miles up the Inderagiri River.

After attempts to head the Carley float eastwards towards Sumatra merely spun the irritating craft in circles, Bird and his companions simply sat on it, their legs dangling through its central void, through the balance of the 15th and the following night. Dawn brought them the welcome sight of land on the starboard bow and in due course they drifted ashore to land on the edge of the vast mangrove swamp which stretches un-broken, except for the huge rivers which pour through it at intervals, for hundreds of miles both to north and south. After considering his alternatives, Bird left his charges seated on mats formed by the sprawling roots of the mangroves and set off northwards to seek assistance. After an arduous journey of perhaps five or six miles wading through the thick, noisome mud of the unbroken swamp he finally reached the estuary of a big river across which he could see a village. Finding a dry spot, Bird spent the night here and the following morning, stripping himself naked, launched himself into the river and swam downstream until opposite the village. After 'shouting like mad' for half an hour Bird was astounded to hear a voice shouting back 'Help coming!' and in due course a man (described simply by Bird as 'an other rank') came across in a canoe, collected him and took him to the village where a Commander Clark RN and a Major Lyddon of the Ordnance Corps were waiting.

Bird accompanied these two men in a twenty-foot canoe searching for a doctor, rumours held was a little way upstream, to patch up Clark whose wrist had been badly damaged by a shell splinter. After about five days of toiling under the blazing sun, by which time Bird (who was wearing only a pair of shorts) had a back which was a mass of suppurating ulcers, they came upon their first sign of civilization since leaving the village, a small hut beside the river in which a Chinaman was living. Here Clark and Bird stayed while Lyddon and the other man (whose name it seems may have been Simpson) continued on upstream. After three or four weeks, two Malays appeared with a canoe and Clark (whose wrist had healed of its own accord) and Bird resumed their passage upstream with them until they reached the river's headwaters where they left the canoe and made their way through a swamp 'black with mosquitos' on a path made of raised tree trunks. After a nightmarish trip they reached a village from which they were transported to a large town (which proved to be Palembang) where they were handed over for blood money to the Japanese.

The fate of the two men Bird had left seated on their

mangrove mats patiently awaiting his return is unknown. It may well be felt that Bird's own comment when faced with the choice of going back for them or accompanying Clark and Lyddon upstream: 'Probably what I ought to have done was to have gone back to the original place where I landed with the two other chaps', was hardly to be disputed.

Donald Wright and his party continued their journey up the Inderagiri in another launch provided by 'the Dutch soldiery who seemed to be very nonchalant about the war, not very knowledgeable and quite *Allah ki fique* about the whole thing'. The trip was memorably beautiful with the river winding through tropical forests with occasional clearings and ended at a small village where the party spent the night before being transported the following morning by six buses to Rengat which was by now an efficiently organized clearing station for escapers from Singapore. Here, the same day, they were packed into old barges which were slowly towed by tugs against the still fierce current of the Inderagiri to reach, late that night, a place called Ayahmolek where they were billeted in an old rubber factory and bathed in the coagulating tanks – their first real wash after five gruelling days in the steamy equatorial climate.

A Colonel Rosenberg now took charge of Wright's party and some one hundred others who had turned up by various means from various directions and, in accordance with propriety, all other ranks were first got away and Wright took the last party in a bus on 19 February to reach, after a hair-raising but 'very, very beautiful' journey with the bus skidding round narrow mountain roads, the two thousand feet high peacetime hill station of Sawahlento at about 2 a.m. Here Wright stayed for a few days enjoying the beauty of the scenery and the magnificent climate before continuing on the 22nd by train to Padang where he was billeted in the old European Club. On the 26th a Dutch river steamer from Java, the *Rossenbaum*, picking up the call for help on its radio receiver, sailed into Padang and collected about one hundred escapers including Wright and, although not a sea-going boat and quite unequipped for deep sea navigation, successfully delivered them all to Colombo which they reached on 4 March.

Wright tells one rather fascinating anecdote. Whilst at

Ayahmolek, in taking a wander through the bush, he came upon a little telegraph office. He enquired as to whether he might possibly send a cable to India and the local native in charge, while pointing out there was very little chance of it getting through and adding that he would certainly not charge for it under the circumstances, agreed to send one. In fact the cable did get through to Wright's family in India and from it they knew he was still alive and in Sumatra, whereas officially, on the Indian Army list, he had been published as missing believed killed.

By the morning of 17 February, less than seventy-two hours since the paratroops had been dropped at Pladjoe and P.1, resistance to the Japanese had ceased. One thought only occupied the minds of servicemen and Europeans alike: escape. For those still in Palembang it was too late – the Japanese were in occupation of the town. For those not heading for Oosthaven or already on the Rengat to Padang route, the chances were now slight indeed. The local population had no particular sympathy for these white men and women who had for so long occupied their lands and it was to their advantage to come to terms with their new masters – and anyway betrayal brought blood money. And escape, meant escape by sea – the country itself dark, brooding, heavy, pestilential, offered no refuge – this was no land for ill equipped and untrained men to take bravely to the hills.

Although a worthwhile number of Allied servicemen escaped from Padang and one or two other, smaller west-coast ports, and there were some individual escapes of great daring along the eastern coast through the Strait of Malacca and thus to India, by far the greatest number of those who got away from Sumatra did so through Oosthaven.

Lionel Wigmore in his book *The Japanese Thrust* gives a total of 6,090 made up of 2,500 RAF, 1,890 British troops, 700 Dutch troops and 1,000 civilians and there seems little reason seriously to quarrel with these figures from which as it will be gathered this relatively modest port was, of a sudden, a hive of great activity in which panic and confusion were important elements.

Hedley Bonnes paints a graphic picture: "We pulled in to Oosthaven and it was a revelation to me, and to all of us I think, to see these beautiful motor cars, all with doors wide open, suitcases strewn all over the street and clothing and expensive stuff just lying about because these people had come down, these Dutch people, expecting to get on the boat and sail back with all their belongings. They were allowed to carry on just one small suitcase on this corvette thing to take them back. We were detailed off, we service types, to shepherd these people, make sure they had nothing else apart from what they were allowed and go and destroy all cars and vehicles. Well the only obvious way to do it was to put a bullet through the sump and run the engine. Most of them had the keys inside so we just let the engine run and burn out.

"Finally the refugees became a trickle and we were told to get on this corvette boat. Before we went though, a lot of our chaps were on the railway sidings which had two or three trains, one particular train with goods wagons and so forth, and some of the blokes had set fire to the coach one or two from the end of the train and they'd set fire to the coach one or two from the start of the train. So this was burning merrily, you see, but these natives round there were dashing around looting everything in sight. Well we couldn't give a damn. The Japs were going to get it all anyway. But, as we went along there, being an armourer and so forth, I noticed that the centre wagons of this train were full of shells: Ack Ack shells, ammunition, bombs, God knows what. All very lethal. So I thought – later on this is going to be a bit hectic when the fire hits it, nothing's going to put it out and anyway behind it was a huge amount (about the size of two good-sized houses – or even higher than that) of petrol tins. I think these were four-gallon tins approx 10" × 10" × 12" also used for tea-brewing. These were stacked up, thousands of the damn things, you know, and they were full of fuel for the aircraft and everything else and they decided they wouldn't blow that up right away it would be too damn dangerous. We told these natives to clear off, to take what they'd got now and buzz off. But they didn't want to hear, they didn't understand English. So with that we did a bit of looting ourselves, you know, fags and things like that and got on this corvette. In the meantime we'd got aero engines and motor bikes and so forth and chucked them in the dock and a couple of Australian blokes had motor bikes on the deck of this corvette.

"And then we put to sea. We were about, I imagine, a quarter of a mile out when the skipper asked any one with arms to open up on this huge dump of petrol. And a chum of mine was on a Lewis gun loaded with tracer and you could see it pouring into this mountain of tins and nothing was happening and in the meantime this train was merrily burning away stuffed with all this ammunition. And I said, my God there's going to be a enormous bang in a minute and suddenly there was a gynormous 'woof!' And up went this petrol. One of our chaps who was sitting on the deck got a piece of tin in his back. And shortly after that the whole place seemed to erupt into a mass of flames and that was that and what happened to those poor wogs, I wouldn't know. Anyway we carried on until we were about a mile out to sea and there was a thundering explosion and the ammo train went up. I don't think there was much loot left for people – or people left to loot. And then we got across to Java."

Taute, who had escaped from Padang, had a story to match Bonnes's. He tells of one corpulent Dutch businessman who came rushing down to the quayside at Padang just as the gangplank was being pulled up. He had a black bag with him which, judging by the way he was listing to one side, was very heavy. He was running and shouting and waving his hat all the way and he just made the gangplank. But as he reached the top, he banged the hand holding the bag against the rail and lost his grip on it and it fell into the sea. And: "He nearly went cuckoo, screaming: 'My money! My money! My money!' Oh he was thoroughly miserable! But in the end it wouldn't have done him any good, would it?"

But perhaps Maguire's exploits on P.1 should allow him the last words – and certainly they are appropriate. Their boat sailed at night and Maguire experienced a phenomenon he had never experienced before and was never to experience again; a phenomenom which, causing much discussion, led to a debate as to what sort of omen it might be and the conclusion, which events were later to prove justified, that it wasn't on their side. For it was the night of the full moon – and the moon was blue.

Epilogue

Although Palembang had fallen and no attempt was to be made to hold any part of Sumatra to the south, by far the greater part of the island, some one hundred and thirty thousand square miles of territory, remained unoccupied by the enemy. The Japanese plans for the taking of this vast area with all the strategic and material advantages such conquest would bring, were as carefully prepared as had been the assault on Palembang. The forces to be used were equally impressive with the crack Imperial Guard Division being assigned the responsibility for the invasion and occupation under the protection of the 1st Southern Expeditionary Fleet.

The plan called for one element of the invasion force to attack Sabang Island and Koetaradja, another to land at Idi and secure the Langsa and Pangkalanbrandan oilfields and the main element to land at Laboehanroekoe and swiftly occupy the important east-coast town of Medan. The combined fleet escorts, again under the command of Ozawa, would be massive and ample air support made available. Monograph 69 gives full, and lengthy, details of the operation and of the units involved. However, the actual campaign is covered in a single paragraph:

"The Guard Division was divided into the Kobayashi Detachment, Yoshida Detachment, Kunishi Advance Force and the main body of the division. The Kobayashi Detachment left Singapore on 8 March, sailed through the Malacca Straits and on 12 March elements landed on Sabang Island and the northern tip of Sumatra in the vicinity of Koetaradja. After securing its objectives the detachment began movement to Idi.

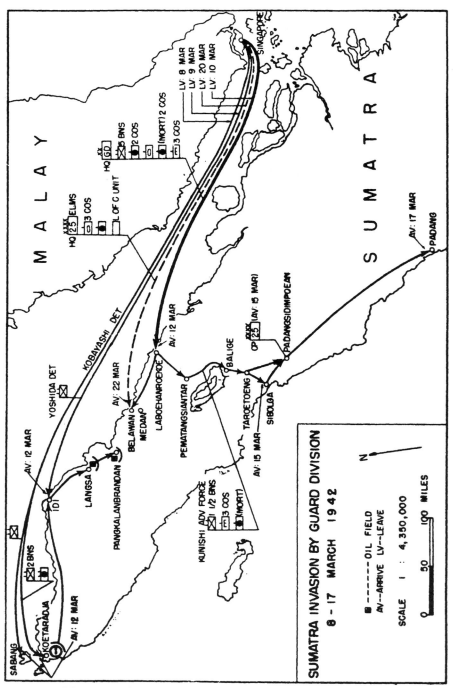

Northern Sumatra showing Japanese invasion plan
which was executed unchanged.

The Yoshida Detachment leaving Singapore on 9 March arrived and landed in the vicinity of Idi on 12 March. After taking its initial objectives, it moved south, occupied the Langsa and Pangkalanbrandan oil areas and continued towards Medan. The main body of the division departed Singapore on 10 March and landed at Laboehanroekoe, 12 March. One element moved north and captured Medan while another element, known as the Kunishi Advance Force moved south towards Padang, which it captured on 17 March. Enemy resistance throughout central and northern Sumatra can be classified as light to non-existent."

There is a footnote, reading:
'The enemy forces in Northern Sumatra numbering about 8,000, assembled and surrendered in Atjehi State.'

Thus ended the conquest of the world's fifth largest island and one of its richest in mineral terms. Java having by this time also capitulated, the strong forces set aside for its reduction were now immediately available for the Burma Campaign.

So far as the Allied troops who had avoided capture in Sumatra were concerned, although a fair number, leaving from Java's southern port of Tjiliatjap, did get away to Ceylon or Australia, the majority were taken prisoner. This, ironically, applied particularly to those who had actually fought the Japanese. Much of my material has been drawn from men of the anti-aircraft batteries, the ground staff of 605 Squadron, men serving under Maguire and from operational pilots – without their stories there would after all be not a great deal to tell. The ground staffs of both 258 and 232 Squadrons were successfully got away but those of 605 continued to service Hurricanes in Java to the very end. The surviving pilots of the Australian bomber squadrons at P.2 had aircraft with the range to evacuate them to Australia. The survivors of 232 Squadron (now flying under the mantle of 242 Squadron) flew the last few fighter planes up to the very day when Java capitulated when eight of them, drawn by lot, including their splendid Commanding Officer, Squadron Leader Brooker, managed to get away by Hudson. So far as my own squadron was concerned,

Author (front row, extreme left) as prisoner of war
dressed in Japanese Army uniform.

"Red" Campbell after
three and a half years as
prisoner of war.

the survivors of a very hectic and unforgettable stint were informed that six should stay behind to form one Flight of a newly constituted 605 Squadron while the rest were to be evacuated to Colombo. A New Zealander, Harry Dobbyn (who was to be killed on our second operational flight from Tjillilitan), was nominated to remain behind as Flight Commander and Campbell and a 'spare pilot', another New Zealander named Vibert who had missed out on the action thus far, volunteered to stay. It was agreed that cards would be drawn to select the remaining three. In a very dramatic ceremony on the stoep of the beautiful Hotel der Nederlanden the draw was made – Healey (escaped from Singapore on the *Empire Star*), Lambert and I drew low.

The surviving 258 Squadron pilots on the morning when cards were drawn as to who should remain to fly the last few Hurricanes against the Japanese in Java. Left to right; back row, Dobbyn, Milnes, Macnamara, Thomson, author, Tremlett, unknown, Lambert, Nash, White. Front row, Campbell, Healey, McCulloch, Cicurel, Sheerin, Vibert, Brown.

There are three questions to be posed regarding the Sumatra Campaign. Firstly, could the initial paratroop drop have been repulsed? Secondly, if it had been repulsed, could the Japanese Advance Force have succeeded in its objective? And lastly, if the Advance Force had failed in its objective, would the Japanese have changed their original invasion plan so far as the main force was concerned and, if so, what would have been the effect on future campaigns?

So far as the 'Raiding Units' were concerned, there seems little doubt that had cool heads and thought in depth from the Dutch command been applied, the attacks could have been repulsed and the paratroops even annihilated. The total combined force of the two drops amounted to less than four hundred men of whom a small proportion would have been killed or incapacitated as the result of being dropped into such hostile terrain, as is in fact confirmed in the Japanese reports. These men were dropped in two groups, the smaller group of one hundred and thirty men close to the refinery where, on the whole, the terrain was less intimidating than that surrounding the airfield; yet this group was clearly held, until orders to retire were given to the defenders. The second group of two hundred and sixty men did not find the way to seize P.1 and only occupied it following Wing Commander Maguire's withdrawal. It is true they cut the Palembang to Djambi road which passes by the airfield but, as anyone who knows the area would confirm, this was not a difficult thing to do. The road was, and indeed remains to this day, a narrow road cut between an overgrowth varying from thick bush to heavy jungle. Any small party from either side possessing rifles, hand grenades and perhaps a machine-gun or two, could have selected any one of a score of locations at which to stage an ambush, overturn a vehicle and block all passage and, as is quite clear from the accounts given by both sides, the Japanese did not in fact permanently deny the road to evacuating Allied troops but did so only sporadically.

It has to be appreciated that this was no paratroop drop as at, say Arnhem, where the troops as soon as they had rid themselves of their parachutes could quickly collect together. These men were largely dropped into thick, inhospitable jungle and although the dispersal between the men of individual planes would not have been great in distance it would have been extremely difficult for them to group together, whilst, so far as batches from different planes were concerned, the problem of even knowing where a nearby batch might be, let alone joining forces with them, was very great indeed.

Even more to the point would have been the problem of supply. There is a limited amount of food, water and ammunition a paratrooper can carry on his person and if he is staunchly resisted he is soon going to need new supplies. In the case of the attack on P.1, and for that matter the oilfield area, this could only have come from the air. Supplies dropped into the type of terrain which, even today, surrounds Palembang airfield, would be partially lost in swamp or high up in trees and such as landed safely would be very difficult to locate. Again, as we have seen from the many accounts, the sheer business of moving around through the jungle and bush of Sumatra presents extraordinary difficulties – swamp, snakes, ants, leeches, jungle, bush, ditches, mosquitoes, lack of drinking water, the tremendous heat, the teeming rain, all militate against planned warfare. Within a matter of a few days, soldiers denied access to proper food, uncontaminated drinking water and medical supplies would begin to succumb to malaria, tropical ulcers, dysentery and other diseases.

So the Japanese had greater problems to face than those opposing them who were on the whole either native troops who were totally at home in the jungle or Allied troops who were, or could have been, entrenched on an airfield with strong points such as around the anti-aircraft guns, behind sandbagged Hurricane bays, or in the terminal building, and slit trenches already dug against enemy bombing and strafing. Moreover the Japanese did not have advantage in numbers although, it must be conceded, they were at the outset better armed and this, to some extent, by the extraordinary decision of the Dutch on the previous days to require the RAF ground staff to hand over their firearms because, ostensibly, the Dutch could find a better use for them.

The small force under Maguire combined with the Maréchausée were, in fact, never seriously challenged. Such engagements as took place were between groups of perhaps a dozen or a score of men on either side and these usually when unarmed men were endeavouring to evacuate, or a party such as that under Taute was endeavouring to winkle out snipers ensconced in coconut palms. Maguire himself states that until quite well on into the afternoon of the 14th 'we were in fact feeling fairly confident that we could repel the sort of attack that we could foresee'. No doubt he was quite right in thinking in this way but unfortunately at about 1600 hours 'a Hurricane flew over and dropped a message which told us that a further Japanese landing in some considerable force was taking place on a river some fifteen miles north of us'. This, of course, was utter nonsense – not only had the Japanese dropped, or landed, no further forces, but it was never in their plans to do so at that stage. The next forces were to be the Advance Force due to commence moving up the rivers on the following day.

Whilst it is perfectly obvious that the reasons for the paratroop drops were the seizure of P.1 and of the oil installations before they could be destroyed, the Dutch command seems to have given little thought as to what would be the Japanese situation should these objectives, and particularly the former, fail. Moreover, as is clear from records subsequently made available, it had been appreciated that an attack on Palembang could only be mounted in the manner in which, in the event, it was mounted – by river and by paratroop drop. Yet the only defensive forces provided by the Dutch to repulse an attack on the airfield were about one hundred semi-military Maréchausée and no real attempt was made to reinforce them once action started. It should not be overlooked that (at least so far as P.1 was concerned) reinforcement from the air was a practicable proposition. The airfield was in Allied hands until nightfall of the 14th and there were sufficient aircraft at P.2 to ferry in enough fresh men to double or treble the defending forces. Perhaps aircraft and lives would have been lost in the process but that is the name of the game in war; but in fact lives and aircraft might not have been lost for there was little air activity from the Japanese on the 14th after the initial protective screen of fighters had returned to their bases – as the Japanese correctly calculated, strafing fighters serve little purpose when both friend and enemy are concealed by a jungle's roof. On the other hand if it was to be considered possible, as it should have been considered possible, that the time would come when P.1 could no longer be usable as a functioning Allied airfield, then surely, with the knowledge that the only efficient way to reinforce and supply a raiding unit was by transport aircraft, at least, as a contingency, the runway should have been mined as was later to be done at Kemajoran Airport, Java.

In their battle orders the Japanese were forthright in their instructions: the main force was 'to attack the airfield and securely occupy it'; the subsidiary force was to 'occupy the refinery and firmly hold their positions'; 'the various co-operating air squadrons will be required of their utmost co-operation *with firm conviction of ultimate victory*'. And therein, of course, lies the reason why P.1 was not held – because the Dutch, far from having a conviction of ultimate victory had a conviction of ultimate defeat. Their minds were to a much greater extent filled with the problem of how to evacuate their civilians, and in many cases their military, to the presumed safety of Java, than with how to devise a resistance at least strong enough to deny the Japanese the airfield and thus leave them floundering gradually to wither away, or be picked off piecemeal, in frightful swamps and jungles. A paratroop drop is a very dramatic thing and imagination can soon build a small force of averagely armed enemy dispersed over a wide area of difficult untracked jungle, unsure of the forces arraigned against them, weighed down with frightful problems of inter-communication and supply, into a seething mass of invincible soldiery capable of, as it were, popping up here, there and anywhere in irresistible force. Unless a cool, unshakeable decision to resist, however bloody the battle might prove to be, was to be taken the moment the drop had been reported, a moral vacuum filled with rumour and exaggeration was bound to ensue. And this is exactly what occurred. Both airfield and oilfield were evacuated not because the Japanese had seized them but because the enemy's mythical reinforcements rendered the defenders' positions untenable.

Turning to the second question – if the paratroops had been repulsed, could the Advance Force have succeeded in its objective? To answer this question, it is necessary to turn to the Japanese records to ascertain what that objective was and this is stated: 'The Advance Force after ensuring the success of the landings (on Banka) was to . . . proceed up the Moesi, Saleh and Telang Rivers for a link-up with the airborne force.' Clearly had the Raiding Unit been repulsed this objective would have been a difficult, although not necessarily impossible, one to achieve – it is one thing to advance for a link-up to a defined rendezvous such as a major airfield, quite another to join with remnants of forces scattered in thick jungle.

Moreover the Advance Force had been divided into three component parts of which one at least (that journeying up the Saleh River) would have found a link-up difficult in any case, for the Saleh winds its way from its lake source one hundred and more miles from its mouth through unbroken swamp. As for the force travelling up the Telang, this had to switch at a junction with the Sebalik River after some fifteen to twenty miles, journey along this for a further twenty and then switch again to the Selatdjaran River for thirty or so miles before joining the Moesi close to Palembang. At no point of disembarkation could any of the forces have found a road before reaching the town itself. In fact the Saleh force, its additional strength not in the event being required, merely switched to the Koembang and then the Komering Rivers and by passed Palembang altogether thus avoiding a difficult march through very inhospitable terrain.

The plan was, of course, never put to a serious test. By the time the Advance Force in its component parts arrived at disembarkation points, all resistance had collapsed and flight was the only objective occupying the minds of those who might have given battle. All the Advance Force had to do was land close to Palembang and make its way unopposed into the open town. Had it been necessary to link up with the paratroops, it could have done so by marching ten miles north along the Djambi road. In fact the reverse operation took place with the paratroopers making their way into Palembang to form the link-up and thus releasing the Advance Force under Colonel Tanaka to pursue, in vehicles which the paratroopers had captured, the Allied forces south.

Let us, however, make the assumption that the paratroopers had been repulsed and then examine the situation from Colonel

Tanaka's point of view. He would have under his control a substantial, but by no means overwhelming force, split into three component parts of which one could only link up with him by an arduous overland march. He would, presumably, be aware that the paratroop drop had failed in its objective and that the airfield was held against him. If he was to carry out his instructions he would have to by pass Palembang itself in order to assist the Raiding Unit before it had been utterly annihilated; if he decided that the more sensible course was first to take Palembang itself, not only would he be acting counter to his orders (a rare thing for a Japanese commander to consider) but he would, through the delay entailed, put the survivors of the Raiding Unit at greater risk.

Moreover the largest part of Tanaka's force, the element moving up the Moesi (which included the Headquarter's Unit), had been severely weakened by strafing attacks carried out on it by Hurricanes, and, later, bombers, from P.2. These fearsome attacks must in any case have puzzled Tanaka for the existence of P.2 was quite unknown to the Japanese although the range of a Hurricane would have been; and, in fact, had he not been advised by radio that P.1 had already fallen, he would have been driven to the assumption that it was still an operational Allied airfield located only a few miles away with all such a consideration entailed.

From this point, one falls into the realms of conjecture not only as to what course Tanaka might have adopted but also as to the the possibility that Dutch resistance might, with the initial attack by the paratroopers defeated, have stiffened. Moreover, on the previous day, Brigadier Steele had under his command at Oosthaven (admittedly some two hundred and fifty miles by road to the south) a light tank squadron of the 3rd Hussars, a British light ack-ack battery and five improvised companies of RAF each with about one hundred riflemen. Even more to the point the *Orcades*, as he was well aware, was due to land no less than three thousand four hundred Australian troops (including the 2/3rd machine-gun battalion under Lt-Col Blackburn and the 2/2 Pioneers under Lt-Col Williams) the next day. And, indeed, the *Orcades* did arrive on midday of the 15th.

A force of such consequence, properly led, should have been

able to handle the far weaker and much mauled companies under Tanaka's command. However, Wavell, acting under the instructions of Churchill only to reinforce Sumatra so long as it was profitable to do so and appraised of the disastrous situation to the north, issued instructions (which were transmitted by the captain of the destroyer *Encounter* escorting the *Orcades*) that no troops were to be disembarked and that the 3rd Hussars were to be put on board and the *Orcades* sail at once. Again one is in the realms of conjecture but, bearing in mind his own statement to Churchill only two days earlier that 'retention of Southern Sumatra [was] essential for successful defence of Java', encouraged by the repulsing of an essential element of the Japanese invasion plan, Wavell might well have not issued such an order. By road, and by train, even by air, holding forces, followed by the main body of nearly four thousand men (of whom the majority were extremely well equipped and whose morale had in no way suffered through bombing or defeats in Malaya, could quite quickly have advanced to Palembang and P.1 and retaken both the airfield and the oil refinery at Pladjoe if they had already fallen.

Given these assumptions, it is reasonable to suppose that Tanaka's modest and divided forces, limited in equipment, denied the possibility of being reinforced with men or supplies via an adjacent airfield, endeavouring in an unknown and hostile country to carry on a campaign whose first essential objective had foundered, could well have been if not defeated, at least held comfortably at bay.

We can now turn to the final and most important two-part question. If the Advance Force had failed, would the Japanese have changed their original plans so far as the main force was concerned and, if so, what would have been the effect on future campaigns?

It will be recalled that the plan was for the twenty-eight transports carrying the main force of the 38th Division under Lt-Genl Tadayoshi Sano to reach the mouth of the Moesi on 17 February and move up to Palembang at high tide. Although subjected to attacks by Hudsons and Blenheims based on P.2, this programme was successfully achieved and the convoy moved upstream to within ten miles of Palembang where the troops disembarked and moved into the town without resistance. Sano, of course, would have known that all advance objectives had been achieved and, apart from possible further irritation from a few enemy bombers or suicide attacks by minor naval craft, there were really no problems to consider.

But supposing none of the objectives *had* been achieved? Sano would be aware that his air cover, and that of Ozawa's fleet, although substantial, would be far weaker than would have been the case with their own air forces operating from P.1. He would either lack the information (which in the event, would assuredly by now have been passed through to him by Tanaka) as to the strength of the forces opposing him or be aware (had Wavell not given his order of the previous day) that these were quite substantial and far greater than had been supposed. He would presume that being by now appraised of what was clearly in store for them, the enemy would have used (as no doubt they would have done) all their ingenuity to create barriers of one kind or another up the Moesi – and it should be appreciated that one or two transports sunk at an inconvenient point could have made the passage of the balance of the convoy impossible. He would know that for all his massive strength, Ozawa would not be enthusiastic to have his fleet hanging around the Banka Strait once having achieved its purpose of delivering the army to Sumatra.

He certainly would have had food for thought. It is one thing steaming in victorious line astern seventy miles up a fast-flowing and tricky river in the knowledge the way ahead has been largely cleared and quite another hazarding an entire division in accordance with a plan which, now that its two earliest elements have gone awry, looks very suspect. We do not know what Sano might have decided; we do not know whether his High Command might have wanted to give the invasion plans further thought before proceeding with them. The Japanese records, assuming total success, are blithely silent on the possibility. Certain it is that the earlier operations were, throughout all the records, shown to be considered of vital importance and that the major effort was very much based on their presumed success. And, as well, it must be remembered that up to this point in the war, the Japanese had succeeded in everything, however daring, they had attempted. Defeat of the

Raiding Units and the Advance Force in Sumatra would have been their first reverse – it is an interesting thought that the story of the Far Eastern War is not of ebb and flow, of victories and defeats following one upon on the other, but of an inexorable forward momentum by the Japanese which, once halted, never gathered pace again.

But probably, even given the annihilation of the Raiding Unit and Advance Force and the strengthening of the defences by the Australians off the *Orcades*, Sano would have proceeded in accordance with his blueprint. Probably he would have still have succeeded in his objectives. But time would have been gained for the Allied cause, the momentum of the Japanese advance would have slowed, morale been boosted. The whole of Southern Sumatra, so effectively evacuated that the Japanese could say of it: 'In Southern Sumatra there were no significant enemy forces. Because of a lack of objectives to attack, the air brigade took over the command, the liaison and the reconnaissance of the advancing front, etc of the 38th Division', might have been fought for instead of the Japanese being able to have two companies 'set off from Palembang on the 16th in commandeered motor cars and dash about 300 kilometres to occupy Tandjeonkarang airfield on the 19th'.

It was not only the Allied command which saw Southern Sumatra as an essential base for the invasion of Java. Time and again through their records, the Japanese indicate they shared this view. Had Sumatra held, for a month or two at least, the invasion of Java would almost certainly have been delayed and, who knows, its total occupation perhaps been denied to the enemy. To discuss this possibility would require as detailed a study as this study of the battle for Palembang and that is not the purpose of this work. But with such a scenario, and by no means an unimaginable scenario, how much easier and how much shorter the conflict which lay ahead for the Allies would have been.

Index